SMART
TEACHING

Sara Miller McCune founded SAGE Publishing in 1965 to support the dissemination of usable knowledge and educate a global community. SAGE publishes more than 1000 journals and over 800 new books each year, spanning a wide range of subject areas. Our growing selection of library products includes archives, data, case studies and video. SAGE remains majority owned by our founder and after her lifetime will become owned by a charitable trust that secures the company's continued independence.

Los Angeles | London | New Delhi | Singapore | Washington DC | Melbourne

SMART TEACHING

A Guide for Trainee Teachers

JULIAN WHITE

Los Angeles | London | New Delhi
Singapore | Washington DC | Melbourne

Los Angeles | London | New Delhi
Singapore | Washington DC | Melbourne

SAGE Publications Ltd
1 Oliver's Yard
55 City Road
London EC1Y 1SP

SAGE Publications Inc.
2455 Teller Road
Thousand Oaks, California 91320

SAGE Publications India Pvt Ltd
B 1/I 1 Mohan Cooperative Industrial Area
Mathura Road
New Delhi 110 044

SAGE Publications Asia-Pacific Pte Ltd
3 Church Street
#10-04 Samsung Hub
Singapore 049483

Editor: James Clark
Assistant editor: Diana Alves
Production editor: Prachi Arora
Copyeditor: Sarah Bury
Proofreader: Derek Markham
Marketing manager: Lorna Patkai
Cover design: Wendy Scott
Typeset by: C&M Digitals (P) Ltd, Chennai, India
Printed in the UK

Library of Congress Control Number: 2021943733

British Library Cataloguing in Publication data

A catalogue record for this book is available from
the British Library

ISBN 978-1-5297-2728-9
ISBN 978-1-5297-2727-2 (pbk)
eISBN 978-1-5297-8884-6

At SAGE we take sustainability seriously. Most of our products are printed in the UK using responsibly sourced
papers and boards. When we print overseas we ensure sustainable papers are used as measured by the PREPS
grading system. We undertake an annual audit to monitor our sustainability.

CONTENTS

ABOUT THE AUTHOR

Julian White is Programme lead for the PGCE in Secondary English at Bradford College. He began teaching in 1996 and has worked in the Midlands, London, the South East and Yorkshire. Starting as a teaching assistant, he taught drama, music and English for many years and worked as a senior leader in three schools, specialising in both student support and curriculum leadership. He is particularly interested in the role of knowledge in the curriculum and how it impacts assessment practice. He has also spent many years working to understand and mitigate for the impact of disadvantage, as a teacher, advisor and, more latterly, as a researcher.

ACKNOWLEDGEMENTS

I'd like to thank Catherine, Evie, Poppy and Finn, whose patience and support enabled this book to happen. Huge thanks also to all the amazing students and teachers that I have worked with over the years, without whom there could be no words.

1

INTRODUCTION

IN THIS CHAPTER, WE WILL COVER:

- A brief introduction to the realities of teaching
- Some guidance regarding the structure of this book
- Three key principles and how they might underpin your professional development
- The position of this book within educational debate

When asked what a teacher does, India, a Year 6 pupil in Hertfordshire, replied, 'Help us'. She was right. What does this mean for you?

You've decided to teach. Well done, you're a brave soul. In doing so, you've taken on a role, as have many over the centuries, that exists to improve lives.

A weighty start, I agree, but let's not mince words: teaching is one of the most important professions when it comes to securing an improved future for our society and those who live within it. By 'improve the future', I mean supporting the creation of happy, safe and fulfilled lives for children everywhere; both in childhood and as they grow into adults, irrespective of background or culture.

It's a significant responsibility. There's no room for you to be anything other than serious about it.

Let's pause for thought and consider the situation in which you now find yourself. You have decided on a career in teaching, you may have already begun or you may be waiting to start. In either case, cliché will be ringing loud wherever you go:

- Teachers work from 9am until 3pm
- They get great holidays
- Those who can't, teach
- Don't smile for the first term
- Buy a jacket with elbow patches

The reality is:

- Teachers usually work at least 50 hours a week (if they're doing it well)
- Holidays are a benefit, but you might spend some of it working
- Highly skilled people make highly skilled teachers
- Smile as much as you can
- Dress professionally, be serious and watch out, patches might come back into fashion

Cliché dispensed, what's the reality? Teaching is an extremely challenging profession, littered with a minefield of initiatives that keep arriving as quickly as you can implement them. However, it is also an amazing profession and the people who choose to work in it are also, overall, amazing too. Why do I make this assertion?

You will be hard pressed to find a group of people as committed to their job and with such a broad range of valuable qualities. It takes courage to walk into a school and then into a classroom of students whose first inclination might be to push all your buttons. It takes resilience to teach and manage groups of 30+ children, hour after hour, week after week, term after term. It takes strength to be under constant scrutiny by your colleagues, your students and the leadership team, not to mention Ofsted, the parents and the press. It takes a certain gravity to be able to listen to people talk about teachers and teaching as though they understand the whole picture (everybody has experienced it and everybody has an opinion), when you understand that the bulk of their assumptions are just that: assumptions.

It takes emotional strength to watch young people struggle academically despite your best efforts. It takes empathy to watch young people make terrible mistakes and appalling choices and then be able to help them to repair the damage. It takes creativity to provide stimulating and rewarding learning experiences with a handful of insufficient resources and a restrictive national assessment regime. It takes grit to engage a pupil with challenging behaviours on a wet, sleety November afternoon, when he has been in detention at lunchtime. It takes emotional intelligence to stay calm and carry on when it all 'kicks off' and you are caught in the middle, through no fault of your own. It takes humour to respond in the right way when the inappropriate question is fired from the back of the classroom. It takes determination to provide the best, when marking is the last thing you feel like doing at the end of a long day.

A person possessing all these qualities, all the time, would make an exceptional leader. They might also appear in a religious text that alters the course of world history. None of us can be this person; you must learn to be forgiving of yourself and accept that you will not manage to sustain this all the time.

That's the grandiosity dealt with. Relax, this is not a grandiose book; quite the opposite in fact. The aim is that this book will be your friend. Whether you are about to start, have just started, or you are further through your early career progression, this book is intended to serve as a 'skeleton' guide to classroom practice. The aim is threefold:

- It will give you a flavour of the reality of classroom practice through drawing on the experiences and expertise of the many wonderful colleagues I have worked with, as well as on some of the latest research.
- It will provide you with several quick, accessible and readily applicable strategies that you can apply in a variety of situations. These will be 'quick dip' friendly; you can access them without reading the whole chapter. They will be contained in the 'Strategies for success' section at the conclusion of each chapter, as well as being considered in more detail in the body of the chapter.
- It will help you to improve your practice by introducing you to some 'guiding principles', which fall under the concept of 'informed practice' and are designed to underpin your development as you move forward.

THE GUIDING PRINCIPLES: INFORMED PRACTICE

The guiding principles referred to above are driven by both pragmatism and moral purpose in equal measure. In relation to pragmatism, these principles, when applied relentlessly, will make you a better teacher and make the job easier in a host of ways. In relation to moral purpose, the challenge is to consider what drove you into teaching in the first place.

Reaching out to and providing for individuals' needs is absolutely the right thing to do. It's certainly pragmatic from a classroom perspective, even if you struggle with the morality.

The need for some guiding principles is clear. Teaching requires broad skills and deep knowledge, particularly in the 21st century. The need to distil it all down to some core ideas, to simplify, is something I have heard being discussed in many staffrooms. Although it is reductive to do so, there is some merit in having concepts to which you can easily refer.

The principles, collectively, amount to 'informed practice'. The idea for this arises from years of observation, professional dialogue and assimilation of research. *How* teachers work is just as impactful as *what* teachers do. This 'how' pertains to a set of attitudes, interpersonal competencies and the attention paid to the pupils as individual people, both when they are learning and when they are not. It can be learned, because it is specific and tangible in nature, and if you do apply it, it will improve your practice. In the 'Strategies for success' sections at the end of the chapters, you will find a subsection entitled 'Gather your information'. This is where the practical advice pertaining to the principles can be found. They also underpin the discourse of each chapter. Let's have a look at the principles now and deconstruct their meaning.

Table 1.1   The guiding principles

Informed practice
Principle 1 It's the learning, not the teaching that matters
Principle 2 Know your students
Principle 3 Teach the students, not the room

IT'S THE LEARNING, NOT THE TEACHING THAT MATTERS

This will sound counterintuitive. It's possible to teach what looks like a really great lesson and for very little learning to take place. Innovative teaching strategies, creative resources, high levels of excitement and engagement can all be easily mistaken for progress and understanding. This is not the same as saying that we don't think very carefully about our strategies – it's just asking us to think about them differently.

Imagine a scenario in which a really competent trainee teacher (Ms Lumiere) delivers a lesson on Shakespeare to a Year 8 class. The lesson involves categorisation activities, in groups, in which the students make decisions about where characters' motivations sit on a sliding scale from good to bad. In the same groups, they are asked to identify key quotations, matching the quotations to the characters. They conclude by writing up some analysis paragraphs together and sharing them as a class.

Instructions are delivered at the beginning of the lesson, with some questions to ensure that the task has been understood. The knowledge required has been revisited and Ms Lumiere has modelled some answers for the whole class. Once the students are working, she circulates the class and checks that they are on task, by asking if they are OK and understand, to which they mostly reply yes and carry on with their work. Ms Lumiere then keeps an eye on the groups to ensure that they remain focused, intervening if any group appears to be veering off the task.

All is fine, or is it? A casual glance at this classroom would reassure a passing senior leader. They would see enthusiasm, high levels of focused group activity, well-prepared resources and a teacher in control of the room. What happens when we look more closely, focusing on one group in the corner of the room?

There are four students in this group. One child, Asif, is confidently taking the lead and organising the others. Two of the others, Jordan and Maddy, are making some good contributions, chipping in some ideas, but submitting to the judgement of Asif and allowing themselves to be directed somewhat. One child, Amy, is mostly silent, but listening for the most part. This plays out for the majority of the lesson and similar scenarios occur in most areas of the room.

There is definitely some valuable learning here about teamwork, cooperation, listening, mutual respect, group motivation, organisation and other such skills, although the students are not given the opportunity to analyse this and are therefore unlikely to be consciously recognising this development. Group work can be immensely valuable at the right time and in the right place; this is not a critique of the strategies, but their implementation and Ms Lumiere's evaluation.

How does Ms Lumiere know what any of this group have learnt? If she spent time closely looking at our group of four, she would see that Asif already knows a lot of this material and is finding it relatively easy, although the explaining that he is doing for others is helping him to structure and articulate what he knows, which will help with future retrieval. Jordan has some great ideas and his understanding is really developing. Talking with Asif and making decisions together is really consolidating his understanding and he is the one that writes the analytical paragraph. Maddy is frustrated. She doesn't agree with a lot of what is being decided and is beginning to switch off and think about other things, although she's smart enough to offer contributions when Ms Lumiere looks over. When Ms Lumiere isn't looking, she's texting under the table. Amy doesn't understand, cares even less and doesn't want to engage with the conversation. When the group write their analysis, she has no understanding of the content because she hasn't engaged. In summary, one quarter of the group is making rapid progress, one quarter is making some progress and half of the group is not making much progress at all.

When Ms Lumiere asks the group to feedback their ideas, Asif speaks for them and does so confidently – their findings are strong and articulated precisely. Ms Lumiere is pleased that the group has succeeded and judges their learning to be a success. She forms the view that the strategies used and the manner in which she has deployed them have secured both learning and progress. She teaches her next Year 8 group using the same lesson format. In short, she focuses on the success of the teaching, as it presents to her, and not the learning. It is a common mistake. How could she have secured a better outcome? The problem is that she has delivered the lesson to the room, not the students, about whom she knows very little.

KNOW YOUR STUDENTS

A lot of the errors above are based on assumptions. Ms Lumiere has assumed that work means progress. She has assumed that a group of students will all progress in the same way and at the same pace. She has assumed that group work delivered in this manner will structure learning. She has assumed that Amy can do what Asif can do. She has assumed that Jordan and Maddy will flourish within the group dynamic that she has set up. The list could go on.

What if she had taken the time to find out more about each student? She might have realised that Asif is a natural leader and that his understanding is significant, but that his writing is often lazy and unstructured. His verbal abilities are masking his output and real achievement. He is popular with his peers and likes to be in the limelight. Jordan is compliant but lacking in confidence. He seldom speaks in whole-class settings, but works hard and usually progresses well. His hesitancy in offering verbal contributions is because he has been receiving speech therapy, as he developed a stammer the previous year. He is on the school's SEND (special educational needs or disabilities) register. Maddy has some behavioural support for anger management, but she is very able. She quickly becomes frustrated with learning, but has shown leadership potential. Outside school, she is the lead singer in an amateur band and a competitive gymnast at county level. Her mother is terminally ill and her attendance has been dropping. Amy was excluded from her previous school for assaulting a teacher when the teacher made her read out loud in a lesson. She struggles socially and has regular counselling. She is a talented poet and short story writer. At breaktime, before the lesson, she was involved in an altercation with an older pupil.

We could reasonably expect Ms Lumiere to have awareness of some of this information, but perhaps not all of it. What difference would it have made if she had known it? How would she have gone about discovering this information? Some of it could have been discovered prior to the lesson, some of it during the lesson, and some of it on reflection after the lesson, for use in future lessons – representing an ongoing cycle of discovery, driven by Ms Lumiere's desire to understand her students better.

TEACH THE STUDENTS, NOT THE ROOM

Let's start with *before the lesson* and posit that Ms Lumiere does some of the pre-lesson information-seeking outlined above. What impact might that have on her planning and teaching? If she had used prior attainment data, school reports, pupil information on the school's system and perhaps consulted some key members of staff, she might have decided that the group needed their roles to be allocated to them.

Jordan, if willing, could be the spokesperson for the group, developing his verbal confidence. Amy and Asif could have been the scribes, structuring the group's ideas for the written submission; in Amy's case, playing to her strengths and building her engagement and in Asif's case, developing his writing and structural skills. Each group member could have been allocated a specific element of the writing to produce. Maddy could have been made the group director, whose role it was to lead the group through the activities, building on her leadership skills and developing her sense of conscientiousness.

Ms Lumiere might also have read the SEND and behaviour support information available about both Jordan and Amy. If she had some awareness of Maddy's tendency to disengage, she might have spoken to colleagues who know her well to understand it in more depth and discover what works for them in helping her to participate. She might have looked at Asif's previous assessments and discovered his relatively low achievement compared to his verbal participation.

During the lesson, Ms Lumiere might have developed a plan for circulating around the room to spend some focused time with each group. She might have been able to respond to Maddy's frustration and Amy's lack of engagement, either within the group setting or through a quiet conversation elsewhere, seeking to understand the reasons for the behaviour, rather than trying to sanction immediately. She might have discovered that Amy needed support following the altercation. In the scenario in which she has adopted the original grouping plan, she might have realised some of what was happening by using some carefully targeted questioning. She could then have reconfigured the roles.

She could have implemented mini progress-checks, asking group members to describe their progress, choosing carefully who to ask in order to gauge understanding and providing careful feedback for them to respond to. She might have built in key benchmark points for each group to reach, at which point they should call her over to share their progress and receive feedback. She might simply have spent some time listening to each group and observing their behaviours. Cascade this out across the room and each group is adapted slightly to ensure that maximum progress and participation is being secured. Ms Lumiere is paying attention to each group and the individuals within it, rather than forming an assessment of the class as a whole.

After the lesson and over time, through reflection on her teaching and through gathering her information, Ms Lumiere might have learnt that Amy struggles with conflict. In conversation with her, she might have been able to offer guidance and support, building trust and Amy's readiness to feel safe in the classroom. In time, Amy might have been able to take on any role within a group and make good progress. She might also have spoken to Ms Lumiere about her problems at breaktime and reduced her tension and worry.

Ms Lumiere might have thought carefully about Asif's writing and given herself a reminder to set him some specific goals in the next lesson to improve the quality of his work. Maddy might have been called back at the end of the lesson and praise could have been offered for the leadership role she adopted and its impact, with some feed forward about how to build on it in her learning. Jordan might also have been commended for his bravery in speaking to the class, building his confidence.

In summary, attention is paid to individual students, lessons are not just delivered to the whole class, and the whole process is driven by a determination to understand individuals, their needs, their learning and the strategies that best suit them. This is what it means to plan for progress and to facilitate learning.

THIS BOOK AND THE CURRENT EDUCATIONAL DEBATE

You will note that the hypothetical situation above describes a lesson in which group-based strategies are employed. There are voices in the educational world that would object to that as an example and would claim that it is the groupings themselves that might prevent progress. There is some merit to that view, and many of the findings from cognitive science at the moment would support it. It is true to say that some strategies are more effective than others, when employed in a specific context. It is also true to say that context, the learners and the intended end-point (an exam, for example) all have a role to play in the judgement concerning the efficacy of any given strategy. Put more simply, strategies and conceptual approaches will differ according to school, year group, subject and stage of progress.

As you progress through this book, we will explore these debates, but will not seek to adopt a stance. The aim of this book is to open you up to a range of possibilities and to make recommendations that are going to support you in achieving Qualified Teacher Status (QTS). There are many authoritative and expert suggestions cited within these pages, and not all of them agree with each other – some are very opposed to each other. This is deliberate and you are encouraged to form a view as you progress through your initial teacher education. Within such a process, there is room for different viewpoints, as long as it enables you to meet the requirements of the *Teachers' Standards* and engage with the *Core Content Framework* (more on those later). You may also discover that some of them are not really as opposed as they might first appear.

The hope is that this book will support you in finding a way to do that. The best way to start applying the thinking in this book is to begin with the guiding principles. Head to the classroom (fire in your belly) and begin the process of noticing, learning, watching and listening to the students in there. Learn about them, inspire them and get them learning as a result. Good luck!

SUMMARY

In this chapter, we have covered:

- Teaching is a challenging profession and a significant responsibility.
- Knowing your students is critical to your success.
- A class is comprised of many individuals. Trying to teach them all the same thing, in the same way, is unlikely to yield good results.
- If you focus too much on your teaching, you will be less likely to have a positive impact. Focus instead on the learning that arises from the teaching: make this your driving concern.
- This book contains guidance that supports you in meeting the requirements of the *Teachers' Standards* and the *Core Content Framework*. It contains numerous perspectives.
- The chapters are designed to support you in recalling the key learning points. Use the tips at the end of the chapter to develop your 'Informed Practice'.

2

TRAINING TO TEACH

IN THIS CHAPTER, WE WILL COVER:

- The common features of teacher training programmes
- How your teaching will be assessed
- The importance of reflection in demonstrating your progress
- Gathering evidence to demonstrate your competence
- Working professionally with school colleagues

INTRODUCTION

Embarking on a teacher training programme, whatever the route, is a serious commitment. Whether you undertake an undergraduate degree followed by a postgraduate programme, an undergraduate programme with a QTS award, or study through an apprenticeship model, the process will be challenging: academically, in terms of skills development and, most importantly, as a developing professional.

THE COMMON FEATURES OF TEACHER TRAINING PROGRAMMES

The majority of programmes combine professional and academic input. The professional input will happen during placement in an educational setting relevant to your chosen phase, while the academic element will depend on your previous level of education. Some programmes, such as Assessment Only, are solely assessed through teaching and supporting evidence. In some programmes, such as a Post Graduate Certificate in Education, you can expect to gain two qualifications: Qualified Teacher Status (QTS) and a Post Graduate Certificate in Education (PGCE). Only the QTS element qualifies you to teach in the state sector, however.

You will be supported by a variety of colleagues. Your provider will assign a tutor, who will oversee your progress throughout the training programme. In secondary, this may be a subject specialist. They will be involved, with other tutors, in the delivery of the provider-based element of your course and may also liaise with you during placement. In a university setting, this might be an academic who specialises in your chosen area (they are also usually qualified teachers). In a School-Centred Initial Teacher Training (SCITT) or School-Direct programme, this could be an experienced school professional.

In school, you will be assigned a mentor, who will guide and support you through developing your professional practice. Both of these individuals will have a key role in your assessment. Alongside these two key roles, you may work with 'host' teachers, whose classes you take over for a period of time. In primary settings, this may be the same person as your mentor. In larger placement settings, you may also be supported by an Initial Teacher Training (ITT) Coordinator, a senior member of staff who will be responsible for all trainees in the school.

As a group, these professionals will deliver the various facets of the programme in a coordinated manner, with each element supporting its counterparts, helping you to develop into an effective, and hopefully inspirational, teacher.

PLACEMENT STRUCTURE

The professional assessment will take place during your teaching placement, which will take place over 120 days (60 days on assessment only). Assessment during placement is based upon your planning, your teaching, your professionalism and your contribution to the life of the school or setting.

The arrangement of these placements can vary, but usually involve experience of at least two settings and at least two age phases. Depending on your chosen sector (primary, secondary), your exposure to different phases may vary. Some secondary programmes may enable you to gain access to post-16 teaching. You will teach lessons, support experienced teachers, undertake observations, carry out research designed to support your understanding of the school, meet with professional mentors and complete reflective processes.

While some programmes, such as a School-Direct training programme, may require you to begin teaching full classes from the outset, others, such as a PGCE or a SCITT programme, may provide you with a more gradual start; this might include a combination of observations, assisting teachers in classes and/or undertaking some specific research tasks that help you to understand the school organisation and school culture in more detail. You might find yourself shadowing a student, making notes on policies, attending a training session or supporting a teacher while they undertake a break duty.

Whatever grading system your training provider uses, aim to achieve the most you can in your training year. There are a couple of very good reasons for this. The first is that the students deserve the very best that you can offer. It's quite a challenge being taught by a trainee teacher and you need their support. The second is that your training year is an opportunity to iron out problems in your planning.

Trainee teachers are given the opportunity to develop their practice in various ways. One of the key mechanisms is the teaching load you undertake, which is significantly less than that of a teacher. By the end of your training year, you can expect to be teaching about 60–70% of an Early Career Teacher (ECT) load. ECTs generally teach somewhere in the region of 18–20 hours a week, so that means about 12–14 hours of teaching, although this will vary according to your provider. When you start your first placement, this will be lower (rising incrementally over time), but again, this will depend on the manner in which your training provider has constructed your programme.

Placements are often supplemented by input from your training provider. This may be frequent and light touch, or it may involve intensive periods during the course of the year. Providers are free to structure this as they wish, so there can be some significant variation, as long as you receive 120 days on placement.

THE ACADEMIC WORK

The academic element will be designed to support your professional development. You may undertake reflective journals, subject-specific investigations, essays, presentations or planning activities. These are normally delivered and/or overseen by a university or college partner. We will not cover the content of these in detail here, as they are so varied, but your provider will be able to offer more details.

The aim of these academic assessments will be to support you in linking theory and practice. This is a crucial element of your work in training to teach. There is a danger, as you undertake the demands of placement, that your academic work may come to be viewed as an additional burden. However, there is significant benefit to be gained from applying yourself to this work.

For example, consider undertaking an essay on assessment. To complete this work, you would need to undertake some reading, which would expose you (if done thoroughly) to a rich history of development in this area. As you read the material, you would discover the work of Black and Wiliam (1998), to name but one example, and begin to develop a deeper understanding of the nature of formative assessment. This would then lead to rich veins of research, during which you would be exposed to a range of different strategies and perspectives that would undoubtedly enhance your classroom practice. In turn, this could then demonstrate that you are meeting the 'Learn that' statements under Standard 6 of the *Core Content Framework* (Department for Education, 2019).

Another example might be a reflective journal, which is a common feature of teacher training programmes. When completed diligently, a reflective exercise can be a powerful tool in the development of your practice. You will literally develop the ability to self-improve. In my experience, the best teachers are those who continue to work in this manner long into their careers, thinking deeply about the impact of their practice in the classroom and constantly looking to develop and improve, to learn and discover things about themselves and wider educational practice. Taking the time to learn some effective frameworks for reflection, with the input of experienced academic tutors and classroom teachers, is a worthwhile exercise that will yield fruit for years to come. Again, this relates to both the *Teachers' Standards* (Department for Education, 2011) and the *Core Content Framework*.

REFLECTIVE QUESTION

- Look at Standard 8 in the *Core Content Framework* and the *Teachers' Standards*. What is the role of reflection in meeting professional expectations?

Your ITT year creates capacity for you to work and think in this manner. As you progress in your career, there are continued opportunities to reflect, study and learn, but you are unlikely to have the same amount of time that is afforded to you in this unique period – so make full use of it!

HOW YOUR TEACHING WILL BE ASSESSED

As well as undertaking academic work, to gain Qualified Teacher Status (QTS) you will need to demonstrate your proficiency in meeting the Teachers' Standards. Meeting the standards is achieved through planning, teaching, assessing and through your professional behaviours and engagement.

Individual institutions will articulate your degree of success in doing so differently: some use Ofsted gradings, some simply indicate a pass, others might have a bespoke grading system. You can use these distinctions in your application for a newly qualified teaching (NQT) post, if you think it might give you the edge.

The *Teachers' Standards* (Department for Education, 2011) are a set of professional competencies. There are eight of them in total, with each one being divided into micro-standards in the form of statements, with an additional 'Part Two' that focuses on personal and professional conduct. Seven of them are concerned exclusively with classroom practice, with the eighth focusing on your professional contribution in the wider school community. They can be summarised as follows:

1. Set high expectations which inspire, motivate and challenge students
2. Promote good progress and outcomes by students
3. Demonstrate good subject and curriculum knowledge
4. Plan and teach well-structured lessons
5. Adapt teaching to respond to the strengths and needs of all students
6. Make accurate and productive use of assessment
7. Manage behaviour effectively to ensure a good and safe learning environment
8. Fulfil wider professional responsibilities

(Department for Education, 2011)

Assessment against these standards will happen predominantly on placement. This will occur during lesson observations, meetings with your mentor and training provider, the manner in which you conduct yourself while in school and through the evidence that you compile to demonstrate your competence.

TEACHING AND OBSERVATIONS

Learning to teach is a process that requires you to deliver lessons to students while under observation. The frequency with which you do this very much depends on your provider, but it will be a feature of your programme. Working with your mentor, or host teacher, you will agree a focus for the lesson and then undertake some planning. Aim to have your plan prepared well in advance of the lesson. This then gives your mentor the opportunity to read your plan prior to the lesson and suggest amendments. Sending a plan to your mentor at 3am, the night before your observation is not likely to result in a positive response and reflects poorly on your professional organisation. If you want to maximise their support, be prepared.

The person observing your lesson will vary. The mentor or host teacher may carry this out, or it may be the Training Coordinator for the school, and sometimes a tutor from your provider. Make sure that they are provided with a copy of your plan (if your programme requires this) and any other additional information that may assist them in arriving at a judgement. This might include seating plans, prior attainment data for the class or resources the students will be using. Be punctual to the lesson (in advance of the students), have your resources ready to go and give yourself time for a deep breath before starting. It can be quite nerve-wracking delivering an observed lesson. Trainees are often particularly nervous when a provider-based tutor arrives, although there really is no need to be so. Everybody wants you to succeed. Even if you don't succeed in fully delivering your plan, it doesn't mean that the observation is a disaster, as illustrated in the case study below.

CASE STUDY: IT'S OK IF IT DOESN'T GO TO PLAN

A trainee I worked with experienced some very challenging behaviour from a group of Year 10 students in an urban, inner-city comprehensive. I arrived at the school and met with the trainee prior to the lesson. She informed me, with some degree of nervousness, that the class I was about to observe could be problematic in terms of behaviour. She provided a plan, which was detailed and very well structured. The resources were excellent. Time and effort had clearly been applied. I was given a seating plan and some prior attainment data. I could see that there was quite a range of achievement. There were also a number of students with additional needs.

The starter activity was projected on the board and she waited at the door for the students, who lined up outside. They were boisterous (lunch had just ended) and she patiently and firmly waited for silence before giving a brief set of instructions about the starter. The class was admitted and she took the time to greet individuals as they entered the room. My presence caused a stir and there was some humour, accompanied by some inappropriate questions. She settled them fairly quickly, including moving some students who had not followed the seating plan. Some needed convincing to comply, but she persevered, using the school warning system, and they did so.

As they were undertaking the starter, almost in silence, the door banged open and a boy entered loudly, shouting at somebody in the corridor as he did so. He was challenged

---

politely on the nature of his entrance and responded with a high level of aggression, questioning the trainee's authority and challenging some of his peers who were looking on in shock. He then refused to sit down where he was asked. The trainee was shaken (who wouldn't be?), but she calmly and patiently repeated her instructions, requesting him to sit in his allocated place. He continued to refuse and the situation escalated unpleasantly. A senior teacher attended the lesson and the boy was removed, shouting and protesting.

The impact on the atmosphere in the room was profound. While some students were shocked, others had found the scenario both entertaining and exciting and were struggling to calm down afterwards. In fact, the trainee spent the remainder of the lesson trying to recover the working atmosphere she had established prior to his arrival. There was constant talking, giggling and a number of students chose to leave their seats and/or call across the room, attempting to discuss and replay the incident further. As a result, only half of the lesson plan was delivered and a number of students learned very little, if anything.

The trainee was very upset in our meeting afterwards. The mentor was providing the feedback and did so with great sensitivity and, to my mind, with great accuracy. The mentor highlighted that the trainee had remained calm and authoritative, both during the incident and during the problems that arose as a result. She had systematically and patiently responded, making consistent use of the behaviour policy. Her responses had been entirely appropriate. As a result, the behaviour was managed to the extent that might have been reasonably expected under the circumstances. In addition, the mentor was able to identify that a number of students had been engaged in the learning and that the conditions created by the trainee had enabled this. There was progress in the lesson, albeit not quite what had been envisaged.

Looking at the trainee's progress over time, I was able to identify that this was a teacher of some ability and tenacity. Her plans were consistently excellent and the quality of her reflections, resources and assessment activity were exemplary.

This case study illustrates that individual observations, while important, do not determine your outcomes. It also illustrates that what might feel like a terrible lesson is not necessarily so. Despite some issues, we were able to evidence some standards being met in that lesson.

OBJECTIVES AND REFLECTION - THEIR ROLE IN ASSESSMENT

Training providers vary in their approach to reflective practice, but it is a requirement that trainees demonstrate an ability to reflect on their progress, identify clear steps for improvement and then act upon them. This capacity for reflection is fundamental to your success as a teacher. The process of reflection becomes part of the story of your development journey; when your final assessment takes place at the end of the programme, your assessor will be able to see the development of your understanding through both the objectives that you receive and how you respond to them.

The Teachers' Standards are accompanied by a guidance document, which states:

> Appropriate self-evaluation, reflection and professional development activity is critical to improving teachers' practice at all career stages. The standards set out clearly the key areas in which a teacher should be able to assess his or her own practice, and receive feedback from colleagues. As their careers progress, teachers will be expected to extend the depth and breadth of knowledge, skill and understanding that they demonstrate in meeting the standards, as is judged to be appropriate to the role they are fulfilling and the context in which they are working.
>
> (Department for Education, 2011)

Let us look at Figure 2.1.

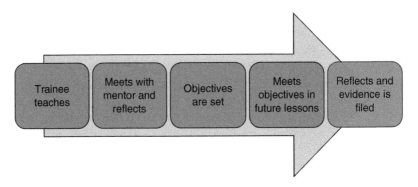

Figure 2.1   The objective setting and reflection process

You can see in Figure 2.1 that reflection plays an important role in your progress. The reflection that occurs in the mentor meeting will be a supported process, but a good mentor will aid you in reflecting on your lesson and arriving at those objectives together, rather than just imposing them. In Figure 2.2, a similar process is outlined, but in this

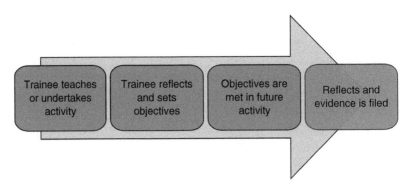

Figure 2.2   Self-reflection: taking responsibility for your own development

model the reflection lies with you, the trainee. This might involve activities undertaken outside lessons, such as participating in a trip or running a club. Being able to work in this manner demonstrates your capacity to develop independently in your professional role, which is a key element of the standards.

The need for quality reflection by trainees is self-evident in both of these processes and is worth us exploring in some detail. Let's begin with trainee reflection. Consider the two pieces of reflective writing below:

> I taught Year 8 today. They were pretty badly behaved and I couldn't get them to focus. My mentor said it's because they come from PE and it gets them over-excited. I couldn't get through my plan and we still had two activities to do when the bell went. One of the students was upset about something and wouldn't participate, but I thought it was best not to push her too much. Some of the students did some work and one of them finished the whole thing, which was good. It was quite a stressful experience and I need to make sure it doesn't happen again or they will fall behind.

> When teaching a Year 8 lesson this week, one lesson involved reading through Chapter 4 in *Animal Farm*. I realised this can cause some students to drift off and not pay attention while the chapter was being read. To prevent this, when reading, I constantly scanned the classroom to determine which students were concentrating so I could target questions to those who were not. The pause in reading for questions also helped me to ensure that comprehension was occurring – some of my questions were targeted carefully to support this. Building this classroom environment as a new teacher with the class has now resulted in students constantly paying attention as they may be chosen to answer a question. This helped to manage the behaviour and reduce distractions in the lesson. I am now beginning to use my questioning to differentiate in the classroom, however, I need to understand specific needs in more detail. Additionally, I think I need to be more proactive about my expectations of the class when we are reading.

You will notice that the second account is of higher quality than the first. The first entry is mainly descriptive; it gives us a clear sense of what happened, how the trainee felt during the experience and there is an attempt to consider the impact moving forward.

The second approaches the task quite differently. This is an actual entry from a Secondary PGCE trainee in the third week of teaching on her first placement. In this entry, the trainee does offer some description, but only that which is necessary to provide context to the reflections. As well as identifying the issues that arose, the trainee describes her attempts to tackle them. She also reflects on the impact of this intervention in terms of student engagement, as well as indicating that she employed a differentiated approach when doing so. She concludes by setting herself an aspiration to improve this yet further through a fairly specific strategy.

In terms of evidencing her development as a teacher, we can see that she is demonstrating progress towards Standards 1, 5 and 7. We can also see that a potential objective might arise from her entry: *design some proactive strategies that foster engagement as a means of pre-empting behaviour issues that might arise.* Moving forward on this objective, she might consider reward systems, use of positive reinforcement, giving responsibilities, outlining expectations at the start of the lesson, and so on.

A sequence of reflections over time, written in this manner, can evidence that a trainee is developing as a reflective practitioner, especially if that sequence has coherence. During the next week, the trainee might attempt to implement the objective and then evaluate her success in doing so. Over time, she becomes increasingly sophisticated in her practice and is able to demonstrate this in both her teaching and her supporting evidence.

Now let's look at the reflection process you might undertake with your mentor. Each week, you will be involved in both formal and informal discussions with your mentor. Who this person is and how their role works more holistically can be found in the section on working with other professionals. One of their key jobs is to help you to determine the next steps in your development. This is often achieved through the setting of weekly objectives.

The objectives will usually be agreed in a professional discussion with your mentor and will be based on their assessment of your progress as a teacher. You both have a meaningful conversation about your current areas for development, to which you contribute your own view, based on your reflection. A good objective resulting from such a conversation might look something like this:

> Aim, by next week, to have used adapted instructions that support targeted learners in your Year 8 class.

You would then plan the instructions, use them in the lesson and assess their impact while teaching. You might assess this by speaking to the students, reading and assessing their work in response to the instructions and gauging the impact on their wider understanding of the subject. Your mentor observes the lesson in which you do this and your subsequent professional conversation critiques your attempts to do so. You both contribute to this discussion as equal partners because you have responded well to the challenge and have applied your reflective abilities in ascertaining your own success. You are able to demonstrate through your teaching that progress has been made and the assessment activities that you undertook reinforce this. You are taking ownership of your own development, supporting your mentor in their work and demonstrating your capacity to move forward.

There are numerous models of reflection that you might consider when improving your practice. Kolb's Experiential Learning Cycle (1984) outlines a process which focuses on novelty. In essence, we identify that which is new or unanticipated in any given experience and subsequently what we might learn from why this is the case. Gibb's Reflective Cycle (1988) is more complex in that it has more stages, but focuses on our feelings about a situation, identifying the negatives and positives that arise and then reflecting on ways in which we might have done things differently. You might also look at the ERA Cycle (Jasper, 2013) and the What Model (Driscoll, 2007). These are both three-stage models that essentially take a new experience, identify learning and then formulate action as a result. All four of these models can be applied effectively in teacher training.

Trainees who do not reflect meaningfully on their own progress become reliant on their mentors for direction, and then, if they achieve QTS, reliant on their colleagues in future roles. It is difficult to imagine an effective or inspirational teacher who is always reliant on the input of others to improve their work. Reflection is a core skill and is based upon your ability to think honestly and critically about your own work and, specifically, the impact of that work on the students that you teach. It's the learning, not the teaching, that matters.

REFLECTIVE QUESTION

- Based on your understanding of your own efficacy, what is likely to be your greatest challenge in teaching and how will you address it?

GATHERING YOUR EVIDENCE

Assessment for QTS requires you to demonstrate where and when you have met the Teachers' Standards. As with nearly everything related to ITT, your provider will determine the best way for you to do this, but there are some elements of commonality in the way this is arranged.

Most of the activities you undertake during your training will afford you the opportunity to progress towards the standards. Additionally, most of them will also be possible to evidence. Let's have a look at some of the ways in which you might do this.

Your teaching will be the easiest element to document. For each lesson you will be expected to produce a plan. Alongside this, it is likely that you will produce resources for the lesson. This might include some slides or materials for the students to work with. Some of your lessons will be observed – the record of this will also be a key piece of evidence. Your provider will ask you to record all these systematically as you progress through the programme. This may be in the form of a physical teaching file, or it may be digital. Coupled with your reflections, which again are likely to form part of your provider's requirements, this will enable you to do the bulk of the evidencing required for standards 1 through to 7.

However, there are additional ways in which you can build up your evidence base. The need to do this will again vary according to your provider. Some providers require a set number of pieces of evidence for each micro-standard; some take a more holistic view. Having said that, it's good practice while training to get into the habit of building up your evidence as you progress. All of it may be useful when you arrive at your final assessment and it doesn't need to be time-consuming.

Let's take a look at Standard 5, for example:

Adapt teaching to respond to the strengths and needs of all students

- know when and how to differentiate appropriately, using approaches which enable students to be taught effectively
- have a secure understanding of how a range of factors can inhibit students' ability to learn, and how best to overcome these
- demonstrate an awareness of the physical, social and intellectual development of children, and know how to adapt teaching to support students' education at different stages of development
- have a clear understanding of the needs of all students, including those with special educational needs; those of high ability; those with English as an additional language; those with disabilities; and be able to use and evaluate distinctive teaching approaches to engage and support them

(Department for Education, 2011)

You can see that this standard requires teachers to ensure that teaching is suitable for all students in the room in terms of accessibility, as well as demonstrating an awareness of the causal factors determining the differences that might arise within groups of children. There is an implication that teachers will build and maintain a significant knowledge base of these causal factors and the strategies that might be employed to support students experiencing them. (A quick sidenote here: this is often interpreted by trainees as referring exclusively to learning obstacles, but you also need to think about those who need to be stretched further.)

Aside from your teaching materials, you might also evidence this standard in the following ways (this list is not exhaustive):

- Notes from meetings attended about a student
- A record of training attended related to SEND or more able students (could be a flyer with some annotation or a record of your key learning points)
- A record of a discussion undertaken with a student outside a lesson
- A photograph of a student's work
- An annotated or highlighted policy
- A record of an observation in which you saw needs being met by a teacher

- A reflection based on a club or intervention group after or before school
- Notes from a lecture or workshop delivered by your provider

All of the above require some organisation from you, but do not necessarily need to be very time-consuming. Make it a matter of habit to think as you work – can I record this quickly and usefully to evidence the standards?

WORKING PROFESSIONALLY WITH SCHOOL COLLEAGUES

Learning to work effectively with other school colleagues will be a key component of your development during your training. Your success as a trainee will depend in large part on the support you receive from experts and on the working relationships that you establish with them. You will become part of the team.

The entire enterprise rests on your ability to behave professionally and the value that you bring to the working environment. This is a really important point to understand. Many trainees do not fully appreciate just how important this is until they begin the placement part of their training. A teacher training programme is not like other university courses. It is a full-time commitment and from the moment that you begin, your provider will communicate that you have made a significant commitment to develop as a professional. So, what exactly does this mean?

Placement colleagues will expect you to behave professionally from the moment that you arrive. This means that your attendance and punctuality must be exemplary; that you are reliable; that you treat all people equally and with respect; that you plan your lessons to a high standard; that you make yourself available and volunteer to undertake tasks that support the colleagues you are working with; that you behave responsibly when using social media, demonstrating an awareness of your new role when you do so.

REFLECTIVE QUESTION

- Which areas of professionalism are going to be most difficult for you and how will you address this?

Your interactions with colleagues form an essential part of your development. You can expect to work with a wide range of people once in school, and some will play a key role in supporting you. Let's take a look at who they might be.

YOUR MENTOR

This will be an experienced Key Stage or subject specialist teacher on most programmes. In primary settings, this is also likely to be your host teacher, whose role we explore below. Your mentor is responsible for supporting you through your training and will also work with your provider in an assessment capacity. You will work closely with them throughout your placement. Please remember that the role of a mentor is often undertaken voluntarily. It may not be part of their substantive role; they may not be given additional time to do it and they also have many other responsibilities. If you experience some frustration that support is not as immediate as you would like it to be, or that your mentor does not fulfil one of their mentoring responsibilities in the way that you would prefer, remember that they are supporting you through this process in addition to their other responsibilities.

Your mentor will meet with you, observe some of your lessons and will set you goals to accomplish that will aid your development. These goals are part of the process we explored earlier in the section on reflection. A good relationship with your mentor is vital. Be available, be helpful and be friendly. Submit your lesson plans well in advance of your lesson so that they have an opportunity to review them and advise you accordingly. Become an asset to the team and you will find that your training and development will be much smoother. There are many trainees whose planning has been of sufficient quality to be distributed to other teachers and has subsequently been embedded in the curriculum. Remember, a placement can be viewed as an extended job interview.

HOST TEACHERS

When you pick up a class, you can expect to be supported by 'host' teachers. These are the teachers who ordinarily will teach the class that you are working with. You are more likely to experience this on secondary programmes, but you might also work with host teachers in large primary settings.

The extent to which host teachers actively support and/or intervene will depend on the individual teacher. Some will stand back, while others will be much more proactive. They are on hand if significant problems arise, but the teaching will be your responsibility. Setting up a good working relationship with your host teachers is very important. During the acclimatisation period, aim to create the right impression: be helpful, be punctual, be proactive, be brave and support the students where you can, if the teaching allows and the opportunity presents.

TEACHING ASSISTANTS

Never underestimate the skill and knowledge of these valuable staff. Many are highly qualified and are highly expert in their roles. Teaching assistants have been through some difficult times recently, partly as a result of budget cuts, but also because of some research that suggested their roles were of little benefit (Hattie, 2009). However, the author of this research has spoken out to state that the research was misinterpreted through superficial reading. What was interpreted as a critique of the role itself was actually a critique of the way in which teaching assistants were deployed by both schools and teachers. A wake-up call for us all. Some really useful advice regarding the deployment of teaching assistants can be found in a report produced by the Education Endowment Foundation (Sharples, Webster & Blatchford, 2015).

Teaching assistants are the best placed people to really support your teaching. If you are lucky enough to work with them, take the time to talk to them outside lessons and find out what they know and what they can offer. They often have in-depth knowledge of the students (not just the ones they are allocated to support) and a high-level skillset in delivering personalised or small-group support. Please don't be one of those teachers who fails to work collaboratively with these valuable professionals.

TEACHER TRAINING COORDINATOR

Depending on the size of your placement setting, you may work with somebody who occupies this role. They have various titles, but in essence they oversee teacher training in the setting. This may involve delivering training sessions, brokering partnerships with providers and sometimes some form of mentoring. Should issues arise during your training, they are a useful contact point and will have an in-depth knowledge of teacher training curricula. Make sure that you make yourself known to them.

A FINAL POINT – IF THINGS ARE NOT GOING WELL

Training to teach is exceptionally challenging. It will place demands on you that are emotional, physical and intellectual in nature. You will be tired, you will experience emotionally charged scenarios, and you may at times feel overwhelmed. All of the people you are working with will understand this. While teaching is a driven and performance-oriented profession, it is also one that is concerned for the welfare and success of the people within it, and that includes you. If you need help, ask for it. There is no shame in telling somebody that you are struggling and then asking for advice about how to reconfigure. If you feel that you haven't been heard, then your provider will always be there to support you. This is a collaborative, socially-driven enterprise: you are not alone.

STRATEGIES FOR SUCCESS

This is the section in which we look at how you might make use of information to support your teaching. Following that, we consider some additional strategies that support the focus of this chapter.

GATHER YOUR INFORMATION

Prior to starting a placement, it is a good idea to equip yourself with as much information as you can about the school or setting you will be going to. You can access information in the following ways:

- Look at the school website. Try to glean what you can about the school's culture and working methods. What are their expressed values and priorities? What are their key successes?
- Look at the school's most recent Ofsted report on: www.gov.uk/government/organisations/ofsted
- Look at the school performance tables and see how the school compares to other similar institutions: www.gov.uk/school-performance-tables
- Contact your mentor as soon as you are able and introduce yourself. Prepare some key questions and demonstrate your interest in joining the school. Make sure that you know when you are expected and where you need to be.
- Upon joining the school, take a look around. What do the displays tell you about the school and its priorities? Take the opportunity to visit other departments and learn about their work.
- Speak to students – what do they have to say about their school? Do they seem proud and how do they describe their experiences?
- Research the local area in which the school is situated. What is the social demographic? Is it urban or rural? What challenges are present socially and economically?
- Research your route for the first day. You don't want to be late.

TIPS FOR SUCCEEDING ON YOUR TRAINING

EVIDENCE 'AS YOU GO'

- Gather your evidence as you progress. Develop a habit of recording everything that will demonstrate your progress towards the standards. Don't leave it until the end!

BE AN EFFECTIVE TEAM MEMBER

- Be proactive. Offer to help. Be happy and friendly. Work hard. Demonstrate your commitment. Teaching is a profession that values commitment to children.

PLAN IN ADVANCE

- Give your mentor plenty of time to respond to your planning. Create time for professional dialogue and this will accelerate your progress.

REFLECT MEANINGFULLY

- Think carefully about your teaching and record your reflections. Don't describe: evaluate. Aim to learn from your experiences and develop.

GET INVOLVED IN SCHOOL LIFE OUTSIDE YOUR LESSONS

- Run clubs. Attend optional training. Get to know teachers in different areas of the school.

DEVELOP YOUR PROFESSIONALISM

- Be clear about what 'professional' means to you and aim to live those values throughout your working day. Behave with integrity and you will be respected.

DEVELOP AN ORGANISATION SYSTEM

- You will be given a lot of information while on the move. How will you systematically record the things you need to do?

MANAGE YOUR WORK/LIFE BALANCE

- Allocate some times each week in which you put your work aside, switch off your emails and enjoy yourself. Learn to relax fully so you can be more present when on task.

BUILD EFFECTIVE RELATIONSHIPS

- This might be fellow trainees, it might be your mentor or it might be staff in your setting, but aim to foster some mutually supportive relationships with colleagues. It makes a huge difference to the quality of your experience.

SUMMARY

In this chapter, we have covered:

- Teacher training programmes vary in their configuration. Research them thoroughly and choose the one that suits you best. All will follow the Core Content Curriculum, but there will be variation in the way in which this is delivered.
- Depending on your programme, you will be assessed both professionally and academically. Professional assessment takes place on placement. You will be assessed against the *Teachers' Standards*, so it is useful to familiarise yourself with these prior to starting the programme.
- Your capacity for honest self-reflection will determine your success in the programme. Trainees who really think about their practice and constantly seek to improve are those who experience the most success. Teaching is not a tick-box exercise; accomplishment in this profession is the result of great subtlety, insight and a desire to learn.
- Gather your evidence as you progress through the programme. Documentation that demonstrates your progress is varied and you will need to be organised in proving that you have met the standards.
- Professionalism is absolutely key to success. Be diligent, be focused, be reliable and, above all, be respectful to all members of your learning community.

REFERENCES

Black, P., & Wiliam, D. (1998) Inside the black box: Raising standards through classroom assessment. *Phi Delta Kappan*, 80(2), 139–148.

Department for Education (2011) *The Teachers' Standards*. London: HMSO. Accessed online (20 December 2020) at: www.gov.uk/government/publications/teachers-standards

Department for Education (2019) *ITT Core Content Framework*. London: HMSO. Accessed online (23 February 2021) at: www.gov.uk/government/publications/initial-teacher-training-itt-core-content-framework

Driscoll, J. (ed.) (2007) *Practicing Clinical Supervision: A Reflective Approach for Healthcare Professionals*. Edinburgh: Elsevier.

Gibbs, G. (1988) *Learning by Doing: A Guide to Teaching and Learning Methods*. Oxford: Further Education Unit, Oxford Polytechnic.

Hattie, J. (2009) *Visible Learning: A synthesis of over 800 Meta-Analyses relating to achievement*. Routledge, London.

Jasper, M. (2013) *Beginning Reflective Practice*. Andover: Cengage Learning.

Kolb, D. (1984) *Experiential Learning: Experience as the Source of Learning and Development.* Upper Saddle River, NJ: Prentice-Hall.

Sharples, J., Webster, W., & Blatchford, P. (2015) *Making the Best Use of Teaching Assistants.* Guidance Report. London: Education Endowment Foundation. Accessed online (20 December 2020) at: https://educationendowmentfoundation.org.uk/public/files/Publications/Teaching_Assistants/TA_Guidance_Report_MakingBestUseOfTeachingAssistants-Printable.pdf

3

LEARNING

IN THIS CHAPTER, WE WILL COVER:

- What is cognition and how does it relate to the development of knowledge?
- How does our memory work and what are the implications for the classroom?
- Which classroom strategies are best placed to support a learning-focused environment?
- Does the way we think about our learning have an impact on learning efficacy?

INTRODUCTION

You might be surprised to learn that, as an educational community, we have only recently begun to pay attention to learning. By that, we mean really questioning where, when and how learning is happening.

Historically, we have framed this mainly in terms of 'outcomes'. School efficacy, and therefore the quality of learning, has been assessed in inspection processes that place great emphasis on outcomes. Outcomes, in Ofsted parlance, refers to a range of things, but when it's discussed in schools, it usually means attainment (results), although this is now changing as a result of new inspection frameworks. We have subsequently assumed (because exams tell us so) that attainment means learning is happening in schools. It is a reasonable assumption, but not one that illuminates the process of getting there.

That process of assumption has been perfectly rational. Teachers have planned lessons and taught with great skill, intending to ensure that really great learning happens. Senior leaders and competent teachers have planned and delivered training on effective pedagogy, then invited evaluation from teachers about their perceptions of the training. Teachers have been invited to share their good practice on the strategies that they employ, because they know best (they do, by the way). We've all been busily focused on the quality of teaching, which makes sense.

REFLECTIVE QUESTION

- Is it possible to do a lot of teaching without any learning happening? What would this teaching look like?

Understanding (and taking an interest in) learning theory has mainly been the province of university researchers and providers of Initial Teacher Training (ITT). Until quite recently, ITT would be likely to include some mention of Piaget, Vygotsky, Bruner and perhaps Dewey, possibly accompanied by some Howard Gardner. Ask most practising teachers to articulate the key ideas of these thinkers and the relationship of those ideas to practice and you would find that most of them haven't given it any substantial thought following completion of their training.

This is not a criticism of teachers, although it may sound like one. The problem is one of relevance. Why concern yourself with dusty theories that don't seem to make substantial impact on the quality of your teaching? Focus instead on getting those grades up, delivering lessons that are as interesting as possible and maintaining order and respect in your classroom – it makes perfect sense within the reality of classroom endeavour. In short, we were focused on the teaching, not the learning. Until recently.

A wonderful thing has happened. Collectively, teachers have begun to seek understanding of the cognitive processes that underpin learning. The introduction of the *Core Content Framework* (Department for Education, 2019) has accompanied this. The educational community is enjoying a new and lively debate concerned with the role and importance of knowledge, the potential applications of cognitive science, and whether we should still be employing a constructivist approach or adopting a more instruction-led pedagogy.

Let's begin by clarifying some of the terminology in this debate. Constructivism, broadly speaking, is a methodology that seeks to engage the learner in actively creating their own learning through carefully designed activities and through engaging learners in collaborative thinking and endeavour, making meaning based on prior knowledge. It draws heavily on the thinking of Dewey (1938), Vygotsky (1978) and Piaget (1932). There are two main concepts here: Cognitive Constructivism (knowledge is constructed by learners, using their existing cognitive frameworks) and Social Constructivism (knowledge is developed through interactions with others). Constructivism, when introduced as an approach in classrooms, revolutionised education. It replaced 'lecture-style' teaching, which positioned the learner as a passive recipient of knowledge. In other words, you were told it, and you either retained it or you didn't. Learning moved from this passive model to a much more active, engaged, meaning-making process. It is wonderful stuff and highly beneficial for learners, in terms of both experience and knowledge acquisition and application.

REFLECTIVE QUESTIONS

- How do the social elements of learning enhance the experience? Can they improve the learning, and if so, how?
- Can an individual construct knowledge for themselves? What processes might facilitate this?

Recent years have seen the development of an approach labelled 'Explicit Instruction'. In my view, this is a misnomer that has unhelpfully contributed to the oppositional nature of the debate. Explicit Instruction isn't instruction as it might have been employed in the early 20th century; far from it, in fact. It does involve some 'telling' (so does constructivism, by the way), but it also involves, as we shall see later, many other stages in which learners are progressed beyond the role of passive recipient. More on that later, but let's think about the debate and its impact on your developing pedagogy.

Sadly, like most debates, this has taken on a somewhat binary shape and the tone has soured in some conversations. 'Sadly' is used here because if you look at the discussion, it seems that both 'sides' are right. There's space for constructivist teaching methods to sit alongside instruction-led, knowledge-focused strategies in the same classroom. It depends on the individual students, the syllabus, exam requirements, the subject, the topic within that subject, the stage of progress and a whole host of other contextual factors.

Language (as always) is being used selectively to frame this false opposition. Terms like 'progressive' and 'traditional' are in some sense unhelpfully contributing to the combative nature of this debate. Instruction-based approaches are being framed as traditional, and constructivist approaches as progressive. It is not accurate to think of the application of cognitive science as lacking in developmental focus and a replication of 'old-school' methodology, just as it is not accurate to think of constructivist approaches as having the monopoly on pedagogical progression. Both approaches have their roots in historical thinking, both are looking to refine the art of teaching.

There is another language tool being used to create this binary. 'Evidence-led' is the new buzz phrase and is used in this debate in a somewhat weaponised fashion. Evidence-led has been adopted by one side of this debate because of the political discourse framing that debate. Evidence-led (meaning those strategies that lead to the highest attainment in a knowledge-focused curriculum) is presented as better.

The idea that 'evidence-led' is better is limiting: it implies the idea that we have reached a point of conclusion. We have, as a species, evaluated the evidence available to us throughout history and developed a whole range of pernicious concepts and practices as a result. New 'evidence' is continually coming to light that shows us the old 'evidence' may have been erroneous. Researchers, pulling together these conclusions, seek to ensure empirical validity in their work, but none of it is bullet-proof. Simply stacking the numbers up does not make a thing the 'whole truth'. Healthy scepticism (itself once a system of thought) is the way in which we continue to develop, rather than blind adherence to new concepts as the 'answer'. Evidence-led does not mean 'magic bullet'. We have not reached the zenith of our potential teaching expertise – we have simply taken another very useful step along the road. Evidence is great, it's useful, it's valid; it's not final.

REFLECTIVE QUESTION

- How would you prefer to learn? Would you prefer to be instructed, guided or left to discover for yourself within a support structure?

You will make your own mind up, based on your research: that is to say, your teaching. Remain open to new concepts, try out new ideas, seek to refresh and innovate, evaluate and reflect with rigour and tenacity, keep reading and trying to understand, look to improve and develop, rather than aiming for some fixed point at which you have become the expert authority. Aim to be a learner yourself – what better way to empathise with the experience of your students?

The aim of this chapter is to introduce you, very briefly, to some of the key concepts underpinning this debate. We will be focusing predominantly on the recent learning from cognitive science, not because we are adopting a stance, but because this methodology is best suited to trainee teachers as you get to grips with securing learning, as it is highly structured and relatively easy to understand. As you develop and progress, you will want to look at other pedagogical processes and extend your repertoire to include some constructivist methodology.

We will look first at cognition, knowledge and overload, with a specific focus on Cognitive Load Theory. Within this section, we also look at memory and its relationship with knowledge. This leads to a focus on classroom strategies, exploring how to effectively sequence strategies so that they support learning. Finally, we focus on dispositions and the role of metacognition and mindsets. Along the way, we will dip into the work of Vygotsky, Piaget, Sweller, Dweck and Rosenshine.

THE *CORE CONTENT FRAMEWORK* AND LEARNING

The *Core Content Framework* (CCF) (Department for Education, 2019) contains the following explicit statements about learning and the role of memory and knowledge within that process:

- Learning involves a lasting change in students' capabilities or understanding.
- Prior knowledge plays an important role in how students learn; committing some key facts to their long-term memory is likely to help students learn more complex ideas.
- An important factor in learning is memory, which can be thought of as comprising two elements: working memory and long-term memory.
- Working memory is where information that is being actively processed is held, but its capacity is limited and can be overloaded.
- Long-term memory can be considered as a store of knowledge that changes as students learn by integrating new ideas with existing knowledge.
- Where prior knowledge is weak, students are more likely to develop misconceptions, particularly if new ideas are introduced too quickly.
- Regular purposeful practice of what has previously been taught can help consolidate material and help students remember what they have learned.

- Requiring students to retrieve information from memory, and spacing practice so that students revisit ideas after a gap are also likely to strengthen recall.
- Worked examples that take students through each step of a new process. (Department for Education, 2019)

This particular set of statements pertains to Teachers' Standard 2, 'Promote good progress' (Department for Education, 2011). The statements in this section of the CCF relates heavily to findings in cognitive science, including the work of Sweller (2011), Bandura (1982) and Rosenshine (2010). It is key to understand the role of memory, the strategies that best enable the embedding of knowledge within memory and those that support effective recall from memory. We will explore this in some detail.

The CCF also contains the following statements:

- Effective teaching can transform students' knowledge, capabilities and beliefs about learning.
- Effective teachers introduce new material in steps, explicitly linking new ideas to what has been previously studied and learned.
- Modelling helps students understand new processes and ideas; good models make abstract ideas concrete and accessible.
- Guides, scaffolds and worked examples can help students apply new ideas, but should be gradually removed as student expertise increases.
- Explicitly teaching students metacognitive strategies linked to subject knowledge, including how to plan, monitor and evaluate, supports independence and academic success.
- Questioning is an essential tool for teachers; questions can be used for many purposes, including to check students' prior knowledge, assess understanding and break down problems.
- High-quality classroom talk can support students to articulate key ideas, consolidate understanding and extend their vocabulary.
- Practice is an integral part of effective teaching; ensuring students have repeated opportunities to practise, with appropriate guidance and support, increases success.

These statements pertain to Standard 4, 'Plan and teach well-structured lessons'. The emphasis here is on process and the strategies that can be employed to support the progress outlined in Standard 2. You can see a focus on the role of classroom talk, including questions, metacognition, scaffolding and modelling (Department for Education, 2011).

COGNITION, KNOWLEDGE AND MEMORY

How important is knowledge? This question sits at the heart of the debate within the educational community and has been a key driver in educational policy. To capture the debate in a nutshell, should we be aiming to develop as much knowledge in the classroom as we can, or are there other, more important learning outcomes, such as skill develop-ment, dispositions or habits of mind that we should instil in our students? Is knowledge the key driver in the learning process, and if so, what role does it play? A further ques-tion then results: should we adopt a highly structured, knowledge-rich, instruction-based approach, or should we be looking to minimise instruction and facilitate processes that enable students to explore, problem-solve and discover knowledge for themselves (constructivism, loosely speaking)?

This chapter will not attempt to answer these questions; you will need to answer them for yourself through reading and classroom practice. It is worth noting that potential answers relate strongly to curriculum and assessment. If these necessitate the storage of lots of information, then do we have a responsibility to support that? What we can do, though, is consider the impact of the key points in the debate on our teaching. One of the key criticisms of the constructivist approach is that it places an unnecessary burden on our working memory, and in doing so, does not take account of our *cognitive architecture* (Kirshner, Sweller & Clark, 2006).

What does this mean? Our memory can be thought of as having two key components: working memory and long-term memory (Atkinson & Shiffrin, 1968). (There is also sensory memory, but that's not helpful here.) Long-term memory is where we store infor-mation for later retrieval – this could be skills or knowledge. Within our working memory are *schema*, the mental structures or categories within which we organise our knowledge (Piaget). Research suggests that this is more or less permanent and virtually unlimited in capacity. Working memory is where we make our effort when we are learning. Working memory is limited in capacity (4–7 new things at once) and is temporary (about 30 seconds). It is also where we deal with new information, prior to committing it to long-term mem-ory. Cognitive Load Theory (Sweller, 2011) tells us that the amount of cognitive effort required to complete a task has a direct impact on the efficacy of transfer to long-term memory and the development of new schema, or new knowledge. The conclusion drawn from this is that the more overloaded the working memory, the less likelihood of infor-mation transfer to long-term memory.

The implications for the classroom are profound. The way that new information is shared should take account of the load placed on the working memory. If we teach in a manner that burdens working memory beyond capacity, we are less likely to secure learn-ing and storage of knowledge. This is particularly important when learners are new to the information being presented. The less prior knowledge that can be accessed from long-term memory, the greater the burden on working memory. Sweller (1988) gives us the terms 'extraneous load' (how the information is shared) and 'intrinsic load' (the inherent complexity of the information). The aim is to reduce extraneous load to allow the great-est opportunity of coping with intrinsic load. Arising from this is the idea that explicit instruction, because it shares information (rather than leaving it to the student to dis-cover), reduces extraneous load.

This is very much tied into the concept of the student as a novice, which in this context has a specific meaning. A novice, in cognitive science terms, means a student who has not yet acquired expertise, in the form of prior, *domain-specific* schema stored in the long-term memory. 'Domain-specific' refers to specialist knowledge or skills pertinent to a defined area of cognition, and is one view of the way in which learning is organised – research continues. If we accept this version, we might conclude that students start as novices, acquire domain-specific knowledge through teaching and learning and that we might then begin to withdraw the level of instruction (explanatory thinking) to allow more exploration in which students make use of their new schema (applied thinking), at which point we might seek to adopt some more constructivist approaches as there will be less intrinsic load.

The implications for classroom practice arising from this are numerous. Essentially, the more complex the material being taught, the more you need to provide support during your teaching. This sounds quite obvious, but it's the means of support that is critical here. Your aim should be to sequence activities in a manner that compensates for the lack of domain-specific knowledge among your students. How do you do this and what should you avoid?

REFLECTIVE QUESTIONS

Imagine teaching somebody who has cooked before, how to make scrambled eggs.

- What prior knowledge would they draw on and what new information would they require?
- How would you structure the process of introducing them to this sequence of tasks?
- How would this be different for somebody who has never cooked before?

SEQUENCING ACTIVITIES SO THAT THEY SUPPORT LEARNING

This is where we get a little technical. The processes that are about to be suggested are just one view of how this might be done. Please don't forget that. They are very much open to critique and scrutiny and there are some prominent educationalists who see it very differently.

The concepts that we are dealing with here are presented separately from two key processes (although they get a mention): Adaptation and Assessment for Learning. The material in this chapter should be assimilated in conjunction with the key learning points from the relevant chapters on those areas. They all sit hand in hand.

We are going to be looking at a process best defined as *explicit instruction*. The first thing to clear up is that teaching is not telling and that 'telling' is different from 'Explicit Instruction'. If teaching were that simple, we could just stand at the front of the room, bombast the students, lecture style, with everything that we think they need to know and forget about the learning. It doesn't work like that, hence our key principle: 'It's the learning, not the teaching, that matters.'

At this point, we can turn to the brilliant work of Rosenshine (2010). If you'd like some more detail and insight into this work, you can also look at the work of Tom Sherrington (2019). Rosenshine based his work on Cognitive Science, observations of classroom practice and cognitive research into instructional procedures. The result is a concise, accessible set of principles that can easily be applied in the classroom. The suggestions below draw on these ideas; there are some modifications of my own, but these don't step beyond the boundaries of Rosenshine's findings.

The ideas can be separated into two strands. We can think of a single lesson or short sequence of lessons, in which we introduce a new concept or a small set of related concepts. We will refer to this as short-term planning. No lesson is a lone island, however, and we also need to think of each lesson as part of a sequence delivered over time, sometimes referred to as long-term planning. Part of that sequence will be returning to previously learned material in order to consolidate understanding and also to ensure retention and recall.

SHORT-TERM PLANNING

Figure 3.1 shows how short-term planning works. Let's work through those in order.

INFORM AND CHECK

In this section of the lesson, you give the students the information they need in order to succeed. This would include the learning objectives (see Chapter 4 on objective-led planning), within which would be contained your explicit success criteria for the learning. Less is more here. Aim to talk in short bursts – lengthy explanations are both disengaging and counterproductive. Work in small, manageable steps, summarising succinctly as you proceed. The 'rule of three' referred to is designed to ensure that you don't overload the working memory. No more than three pieces of information at any one time is a helpful way to ensure this.

If you can link the new knowledge to previous knowledge, this will strengthen acquisition of schema. This is known as an *advance organiser* (Ausubel, 1960). For example, when teaching the concept of ratio, you might make use of fractions to explain the concept of a relationship between two numbers.

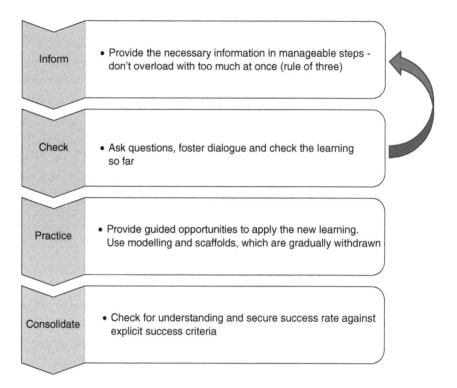

Figure 3.1   Sequencing activities to secure new learning

Dual Coding Theory (Clark & Paivio, 1991) provides us with some really valuable guidance for this stage of proceedings. It seems that the adage 'A picture speaks a thousand words' is actually true when it comes to cognition and learning. Carefully selected imagery that illustrates a concept cleanly, supported by meaningful discussion, is much better than a slide with text on it, which you are likely to just read out in any event. This is a very basic explanation of this concept, so please do take the time to explore it further, starting with the cited article.

You will note that Figure 3.1 indicates a looped relationship between the 'inform' and 'check stages'. As you introduce those bite-sized chunks of information, check for understanding before proceeding to the next piece of information that the students need. This also provides an opportunity for you to break up your explanations as well.

Asking questions is a key, multi-functional skill to develop in your teaching – there's so much information on how to do this well, it could be a book of its own. In this context, we're using it to check. Depending on the level of prior knowledge, the checking can be explanatory, applied or critical, and some examples are provided in Chapter 4 on objective-led planning. Questions can be used to check for understanding and explain (explanatory,) clarify (explanatory), compare (applied), select from options and explain (applied), justify (critical), evaluate (critical) – the list is very long. Use the stems in the chapter to help you to get started. We will look at the role of questioning in fostering dialogue in the next section.

PROVIDE GUIDED OPPORTUNITIES TO APPLY THE LEARNING

The key to this is modelling, scaffolds and eventual withdrawal of dependence on your teaching.

For example, imagine a secondary computer science lesson. The teacher has explained the coding sequence that the students are learning about and its application in designing a graphic. The basic coding language and structure has been shared. The teacher has checked that some of the key principles have been assimilated, but the students are not yet ready to work with it independently. The teacher writes some code, which is displayed on the whiteboard, demonstrating, through modelling, how to use it – narrating their thinking as they do so (which shares their expert insight).

The next stage is to partially withdraw the scaffold. The teacher displays some partially completed code, and through discussion, questions and agreement, works with the class to complete it with them. The next stage might involve students completing a small section of coding independently, or they might be given a partially completed one to finalise.

This stage also relates precisely to our 'three-tier-thinking' model (TTT model, see Chapter 4). The emerging research shows that creating opportunities to apply new knowledge (once domain-specific information is adequately secured) strengthens schema and facilitates future recall. This is the point at which you can make use of applied thinking.

SECURE SUCCESS

Monitoring carefully, the teacher decides the point at which the scaffold can be completely withdrawn and the students can work independently with a high level of success. To do so, the teacher will need to use carefully designed assessment strategies (see Chapter 7 on assessment). Rosenshine (2010) and Sherrington (2019) both emphasise that checking for understanding amounts to more than just asking a couple of students if they have understood, then assuming that the rest of the class have understood in exactly the same way. We need to be much more forensic than that, and you should aim to begin the process as early as possible, giving yourself maximum opportunity to gauge what has been learned. Don't move on until you're confident that the success criteria that you identified at the outset have been met. Be prepared to be flexible in responding to the needs of your students as they arise. Assessment for learning and adaptation sit hand in hand here.

Implicit in this is the need for some tightly articulated success criteria, ideally with the means of assessment embedded within this articulation. Our chapter on objective-led planning (Chapter 4) covers this in some detail.

LONG-TERM PLANNING

Having covered short-term, or single-lesson planning, we now look at how this discrete section of learning will form part of a larger sequence of activities, lessons and topics. This is the wider curriculum within which the learning sits, carefully placed. Within this chapter, we will not be looking at how the curriculum is structured and the reasons for that, but we will focus briefly on how lesson planning can ensure that information learned at different points in time can be revisited in order to support retrieval.

Rosenshine (2010) breaks this into two separate components: 'Daily Review' and 'Weekly or Monthly Review'. If you would like to find out more about this and develop your understanding, then the work of Kate Jones (2019) is proving to be popular among teachers at the moment.

Rosenshine suggests that lessons should begin with a daily review of previous learned material. He suggests that it should be quite short and ideally have some relevance to the material being taught that day (triggering prior knowledge). It could include recall activities, summaries, going over particularly difficult concepts, addressing misconceptions found in marked work or to engage in overlearning (moving students firmly beyond the point of mastery).

Weekly or monthly reviews, he suggests, should be systematic, scheduled and prioritised. Doing so strengthens schema, allows for patterns between strands of knowledge to be recognised and consolidated, thus reducing the cognitive load and strain on working memory. There is a caveat with this – it shouldn't mean frequent, high-stakes testing. This eats into learning time, creating unnecessary and additional stress. A school I worked in ran formal, exam-like assessments every four weeks with the intention of acclimatising students to the exam experience. It didn't. They were just as stressed (if not more) at exam time as students in other schools where this didn't happen.

The concept of 'low-stakes testing' has now formed part of the dialogue. Look to review in a way that is celebratory, non-inspectorial, supportive and diagnostic. Use it as an opportunity to highlight to students how well they are doing in retaining their learning. Make the gaps that you uncover part of the learning journey, rather than something undesirable.

Testing, of course, is not the only way to review, although it can be useful. There are lots of engaging, quick ways in which you might support students in checking their own knowledge. These might include demonstrations, short presentations, debates, mind-maps or graphic organisers, to mention a few. Don't overburden yourself with marking it all – the aim is for students to ascertain for themselves where the gaps are, so they can do better next time!

Most of the material covered in this section can be categorised as techniques involved in *Explicit Instruction* and are maximally beneficial for the trainee teacher at the beginning of their career. As discussed at the outset of the chapter, there are other approaches, and these approaches also have value; they are not mutually exclusive. Constructivist approaches, such as problem-solving, group project work, presentations and research tasks are processes in which the student makes meaning for themselves through a process of supported discovery, social interaction and independent meaning-making. There is room for this kind of facilitative approach in the later stages of the learning, once the knowledge upon which it relies has been secured. Such approaches can be excellent methods for securing the kind of outcomes aspired to in the latter two stages of our three-tier-thinking model: applied and critical thinking.

That covers some of the processes that you might employ in constructing your lesson plans. Let's look now at additional processes that you might employ in supporting your students to develop an awareness of their own learning.

LEARNING AND METACOGNITION

I recently asked a trainee teacher, Lizzy, about how she would approach an assignment at Master's level. She chuckled and suggested that there were two answers to the question – the one she'd like to give and the truth. The truth sounded something like this:

> I will do a bit of reading around, but there won't be much of a sense of urgency. I might try to access some examples of similar work so I can get a sense of where I'm heading, as I find this supports me with structure and provides further focus for my reading. I do all the reading first and organise it under headings, which gives me further structure. I won't really begin doing the writing until the deadline is quite close, at which point I will discover that if I had more time, I will do a better job. I nearly always do this and have been working to make sure that I start a bit earlier each time, using this realisation as a sort of motivator. I try to leave enough time for a deep edit, I'm prone to grammar errors and rambling sentences that I only notice when some time has passed after the writing – it's like I read what I expect to if I don't leave enough space between writing and checking. Even then, I get my partner to proof-read it again, as I still feel nervous that I've missed things.

Lizzy has employed a metacognitive approach to completing her assignment. What exactly does that mean, though? If we look at her reflections, she shows awareness of her strengths and areas for development. She has some clearly defined strategies for success, including a process which is still in development; it's in development because of her motivational struggles, but she has full awareness of this and its impact. She also shows awareness of the role of her emotional states in securing success. In other words, she's an effective learner who is looking to improve further.

She is employing processes and behaviours that support her current and future efficacy in learning. The processes are reflective, based on her experiences. She has taken the time to learn from her previous successes and difficulties and has used these reflections to shape her current approach. The behaviours are self-knowing and self-regulatory: she knows those behaviours that she needs to work on and those which can be employed to her benefit.

REFLECTIVE QUESTION

- What is your own approach to effective learning? How do you organise yourself? Which strategies are most successful in supporting your recall?

These are the signifiers of an effective learner and are quite separate from notions of ability. We all know the quick learner who is consistently outstripped by the slower learner who is diligent, organised, proactive, reflective and motivated. The likelihood is that the slower learner has excellent metacognitive processes in place.

To be metacognitive, we need to have an awareness of our cognition. Cognition is the methodology that we employ in our learning. This might be use of a mnemonic, or a specific method for long division, or arranging information using a graphic organiser. Metacognition amounts to our awareness of these strategies and the efficacy of their use for us as individual learners. The strength of the relationship between cognition and metacognition is underpinned by our motivation to form links between the two.

John Hattie, in his seminal work, *Visible Learning for Teachers* (2012: 266), ranks metacognitive strategies at 14th (out of 150) in his list of 'influences on achievement', with an effect size of 0.68. The Education Endowment Foundation's own measurements indicate a range of outcomes as high as 0.9 (Education Endowment Foundation, 2020). Simply put, that means it works and we should all be encouraging it.

The excellent news at this point is that teachers (you) can support students in becoming better at these processes. Your role, according to the research, is clear. It's essentially about adding an extra layer to the teaching and the learning. If you do this, you can support students in developing three key areas of metacognition that will help them to actually improve as learners. The three areas are:

- Self-monitoring – paying attention to and learning from their successes and obstacles, noticing which processes work and which don't

- Self-regulation – paying attention to, learning from and acting upon their emotional responses, decisions and motivations related to learning
- Self-efficacy – paying attention to and learning from perceptions about their own ability

Bandura (1982) provides us with the concept of 'self-efficacy'. This is the important one. If we build up a perception of ourselves as effective learners, based upon an informed understanding of our successes and failures, we are going to experience greater success in our learning. Students who are described as challenging, or difficult to teach, or unmotivated often have a low sense of self-efficacy. If we berate them for this, all we do is then fuel that negative perception.

What then, can we actually do to support this process? First, familiarise yourself with some of the thinking. The Education Endowment Foundation (2020) has produced an excellent guide for teachers that will support you in developing practically. Zimmerman's (1989) article on self-regulation underlines the impact of environmental factors on self-regulation. As the engineer of the learning environment, the implications for teachers are profound.

Look to make metacognition an embedded part of your classroom practice. Do this by providing opportunities to discuss processes. For example, if teaching Year 8 how to analyse historical sources, hold a conversation about the type of reading they do. Pose the question about the relative efficacy of skimming, scanning or deep reading. Which is most effective? Is the answer the same for each student? How have they noted down their findings? Have some done it in a list, others in a flowchart and others on a mind-map? Why did they make these choices? What do we learn from this moving forward?

Look to support students with self-regulation. If you see a student with their head down, ask yourself why. Rather than challenging this as a behaviour issue, look to adapt your teaching by encouraging them to explore their lack of motivation. What is it about this task that's causing them to respond in this manner? Is there an approach that they would find more helpful?

When modelling how to approach problems or questions, create a meta-narrative. Explain your reasoning, talk about why you are making particular decisions, ask them about your decisions (why have I just done that?). Look at alternative approaches and ask them to compare the effectiveness.

The level of challenge you set is of paramount importance. You will learn to pitch the work so that you are in Vygotsky's 'Zone of Proximal Development' (1978). Essentially put, this means that they are in the area of learning at which they can just about cope with minimal input from you; in this theoretical model, 'you' being the 'more knowledgeable other'. If the learning is too hard, negative emotional responses are likely to result and you might experience some behaviour issues. If it's too easy, the same might occur. This is why it is so essential to do your research and ensure that, even (perhaps especially) with a new class, you know your students.

Finally, look to be explicit about metacognition. Build structured and explicitly sig-nalled processes into activities that enable students to plan their approach to learning, relate the learning to their previous knowledge and then evaluate how well they have done. Create talk around this so that all can learn about what works, how the learning sits within the wider picture and how successful they have been.

As you look to foster their independence and support them in building a positive sense of their own efficacy, carefully withdraw your scaffolds, signalling that it's happening as you do so and celebrating their growing lack of reliance upon your guidance. Feedback on their efforts and invite them to self-assess, using explicit success criteria. Enable them to identify their success, why this success has occurred and which processes have been instrumental in securing it.

All of this will help them to develop something called a 'growth mindset', an idea first developed by Carol Dweck (2006). There has been a great deal of misunderstanding in relation to this work, the main one being that potential is everything and if we just believe it, we can do just about anything. This is clearly not the case and telling students this is unhelpful. We discuss notions of ability in Chapter 6 on adaptive teaching. While it is unhelpful to adapt in a way that creates boundaries or imposes limitation, the reality is that we don't all have the capacity to become nuclear physicists or Grand Masters in chess: we do have limitations.

There is one very uplifting message from Dweck's work, though, which resonates loudly with metacognition and the development of learning skill: if a person works on their sense of self-efficacy and believes that it will improve, this in turn will expand their capacity to become more effective. Essentially, we increase our potential by believing that we can. What Dweck and Leggett (1988) found is that people's attitude to their own intelligence, and therefore their sense of self-efficacy, can impact on their success in learn-ing. People with an 'entity theory of intelligence' believe that their intelligence is a fixed quality; it cannot grow. On the other hand, people with an 'incremental theory of intel-ligence' perceive that their intelligence can be expanded as a result of hard work.

Although some studies have taken this idea on and found results of varying quality, including one quite damning piece of research by the Education Endowment Foundation (2019), it doesn't detract from a key principle which might underpin your teaching – no student should simply be defined as the sum total of their previous achievements. Support them in developing their sense of self-efficacy and you are very likely to see improvement; do so by developing a metacognitive classroom in which the culture is one of open pos-sibility, possibility that is achieved through embracing challenge (Dweck & Leggett, 1988).

Additionally, look to create a classroom that is based on learning rather than per-formance outcomes. Rather than focusing on grade-based achievements, look to chart progress against learning objectives. Instead of celebrating the achievement of high grades, look to acknowledge where the learning has happened: what vocabulary has been mastered; which mathematical process is now demonstrably fluid; the quality and depth of an explanation; the speed and accuracy with which translation is accomplished; the comprehensive inclusion of key pieces of information. This cannot be done without working closely with individuals, getting to know them as human beings and working to teach the students, not the room.

STRATEGIES FOR SUCCESS

This is the section in which we look at how you might make use of information to support your teaching. Following that, we consider some additional strategies that support the focus of this chapter.

GATHER YOUR INFORMATION

BEFORE THE LESSON

This chapter has focused on the strategies that you can use to help your students develop their knowledge, skills and understanding in your subject. Consequently, we will now focus on how you can build your understanding of a class prior to teaching them and, specifically, what they know and don't know.

When you pick up a class on placement, in all likelihood you will be starting to teach them at a midway point in a topic. You need to understand what they have covered already and what remains to be covered. You need to understand their level of success in assimilating the new knowledge so that you can choose material and pitch information at the right level to support their progress. Look through their existing work. This might be in exercise books or they may have completed assessments. Try to gain a picture of both the individuals and the group. Is there a significant range in their achievement thus far and what does this mean in terms of your planning for adaptations?

Look at their prior attainment data in the subject. Use both their school reports and any available departmental or class teacher data. How well did they do on their previous assessment? If you look further back, is the pattern of achievement the same in every topic, or on every school report, as it is in the most recent assessment? Look for anomalies. Have students underachieved in some topics, but not in others?

Access any information relating to additional needs. Use the school's SEND information to ensure that your planned adaptations meet individual needs and think about how these will fit within your sequenced activities.

Speak to colleagues. Ask about both the group and specific individuals. Which students are likely to struggle with your proposed planning? What adaptations might be required? Who might benefit from some additional explanation or some one-to-one support? Which activities have worked well with this group historically, and which might you be well advised to avoid?

(Continued)

Look at how others have approached the material. Access lesson plans and resources online (but do so critically). Speak to other teachers of your subject or year group. Which strategies have been most successful? Will these strategies transfer well to the profile of the group that you are planning to teach?

DURING THE LESSON

Pay really close attention to all the students. Try to ascertain who has learnt what – focus on this relentlessly and adapt your teaching in response.

AFTER THE LESSON

Reflect on the learning that took place. Who learnt what and how do you know? Make notes and consider the implications for future lessons.

Reflect on your chosen strategies. Were there any 'sticking points' during the lesson when the students seemed to struggle? Conversely, at which points did the learning seem to accelerate. What conclusions can you draw from this for further teaching?

What metacognitive developments took place? Did you manage to implement meta-cognitive talk at key stages in the lesson? Did the students articulate any conclusions that suggest an increase in self-efficacy or self-regulation? Were these noted? Are there implications for following up in the next lesson?

Were there any elements of the learning that were likely to benefit from a review process? When and how will you do this? What plans will you create to repeat this process?

TIPS FOR EFFECTIVE LEARNING

IT'S THE LEARNING, NOT THE TEACHING, THAT MATTERS

- As you plan strategies, don't plan to teach the material, plan for the learning – where and how will it happen and how will you know?

KNOW YOUR STUDENTS

- Use prior attainment and assessment for learning to build your understanding of individual progress.

DELIVER INFORMATION IN BITE-SIZED, MANAGEABLE CHUNKS

- Cognitive Load Theory tells us that we can easily overload students. No more than three pieces of information at one time. Keep teacher-talk concise.

CREATE OPPORTUNITIES FOR NEW KNOWLEDGE TO BE APPLIED

- Our short-term memory is limited in capacity. We quickly forget information if we are not given the opportunity to make use of it.

CHECK FOR UNDERSTANDING AS YOU PROGRESS

- Don't move on to new material until you have successfully secured understanding from all students.

MODELLING IS A HIGHLY EFFECTIVE STRATEGY FOR SECURING LEARNING

- Explicitly demonstrate how to do things. Verbalise your own thinking as you do so and give them the perspective of the expert.

QUESTIONING IS A KEY TEACHER SKILL. PLAN YOUR QUESTIONS IN ADVANCE FOR KEY STAGES OF THE LESSON

- Use the three-tier-thinking (TTT) model to plan questions that check for understanding. Personalise these for students according to their progress.

LOOK TO REVIEW LEARNING AT THE START OF LESSONS

- Plan this carefully. What learning will you review and how many times will you review it? Build this into your short-term and long-term planning.

SCAFFOLDING, GRADUALLY WITHDRAWN, SUPPORTS INDEPENDENCE

- Independence is best fostered through carefully pitched support. Carefully consider at which point you will withdraw support structures. Base this on their demonstrable success.

AIM TO MAKE THE LEARNING CHALLENGING

- Pitch the learning so that students are stretched, creating 'desirable difficulty' and working at the edge of their learning capacity.

(Continued)

CREATE METACOGNITIVE TALK OPPORTUNITIES

- Explicit opportunities for students to self-monitor and identify successful strategies will increase their learning efficacy over time.

ENABLE STUDENTS TO BUILD THEIR SENSE OF SELF-EFFICACY

- Having faith that we can improve increases our capacity for improvement. Talk to students in a way that reinforces this message. Small improvements can lead to big improvements over time.

SUMMARY

In this chapter, we have covered:

- Cognition refers to the processes in our brain that are employed as we acquire new knowledge or skills. Some strategies support these processes better than others. The more knowledge we have available about a specific domain, the more effective we are at assimilating new knowledge in relation to it.
- Our memory has two key components: short-term memory and long-term memory. Our short-term memory is transient, finite and easily overloaded. In order to transfer new knowledge to our long-term memory, we need to apply it, with support.
- There is room for both Explicit Instruction and Constructivist learning in an effective classroom. Explicit Instruction is particularly useful for unfamiliar concepts or processes, as it can provide the scaffolds needed to avoid cognitive overload. The level of challenge must be very carefully pitched to accommodate this and facilitate maximum retention.
- Helping students to develop a metacognitive approach to their learning can increase their ability to self-regulate and their sense of self-efficacy; this in turn will impact positively on both their potential (by increasing it) and their learning (by improving it).

REFERENCES

Atkinson, R. C., & Shiffrin, R. M. (1968) Human memory: A proposed system and its control processes. In K. W. Spence & J. T. Spence (eds), *The Psychology of Learning and Motivation* (Volume 2, pp. 89–195). New York: Academic Press.

Ausubel, D. P. (1960) The use of advance organisers in the learning and retention of meaningful verbal material. *Journal of Educational Psychology*, 51, 267–272.

Bandura, A. (1982) Self-efficacy mechanism in human agency. *American Psychologist*, 37(2), 122–147.

Clark, J. M., & Pavio, A. (1991) Dual coding theory and education. *Educational Psychology Review*, 3(3), 149–210.

Department for Education (2011) *Teachers' Standards*. London: HMSO. Accessed online (23 February 2021) at: www.gov.uk/government/publications/teachers-standards

Department for Education (2019) *ITT Core Content Framework*. London: HMSO. Accessed online (23 February 2021) at: www.gov.uk/government/publications/initial-teacher-training-itt-core-content-framework

Dewey, J. (1938) *Experience and Education*. New York: Collier Books.

Dweck, C. S. (2006) *Mindset: How You Can Fulfil Your Potential*. New York: Random House.

Dweck, C. S., & Leggett, E. L. (1988) A social-cognitive approach to motivation and personality. *Psychological Review*, 95, 256–273.

Education Endowment Foundation (2019) *Changing Mindsets*. London: EEF. Accessed online (26 May 2021) at: https://educationendowmentfoundation.org.uk/projects-and-evaluation/projects/changing-mindset-2015/

Education Endowment Foundation (2020) *Metacognition and Self-Regulation Review*. London: EEF. Accessed online (26 May 2021) at: https://educationendowmentfoundation.org.uk/tools/guidance-reports/metacognition-and-self-regulated-learning/

Hattie, J. (2012) *Visible Learning for Teachers: Maximising Impact on Learning*. Abingdon: Routledge.

Jones, K. (2019) *Retrieval Practice: Research and Resources for Every Classroom*. Woodbridge: John Catt Educational.

Krishner, P. A., Sweller, J., & Clark, R. E. (2006) Why minimal guidance during instruction does not work: An analysis of the failure of constructivist, discovery, problem-based, experiential, and inquiry-based teaching. *Educational Psychologist*, 41(2), 75–86.

Piaget, J. (1932) *The Moral Judgement of the Child*. London: Routledge.

Rosenshine, B. (2010) Principles of Instruction. The International Academy of Education (IAE) *Educational Practices* Series 21. London: IAE.

Sherrington, T. (2019) *Rosenshine's Principles in Action*. Woodbridge: John Catt Educational.

Sweller, J. (1988) Cognitive load during problem solving: Effects on learning. *Cognitive Science*, 12(2), 257–285.

Sweller, J. (2011) *Cognitive Load Theory*. New York: Springer.

Vygotsky, L. S. (1978) *Mind in Society: The Development of Higher Psychological Processes*. Cambridge, MA: Harvard University Press.

Zimmerman, B. J. (1989) A social cognitive view of self-regulated academic learning. *Journal of Educational Psychology*, 81, 329–339.

OBJECTIVE-LED PLANNING

INTRODUCTION

How you plan, the level of time you invest and the detail you need will change as you build your expertise. Trainee teachers spend a lot of time planning and you will find that it can take quite some time when you first embark on the process. It does get quicker as you build your skill. You will also find that you become adept at adapting materials you have used previously in order to reduce planning time.

A report by the Sutton Trust (Coe et al., 2014) found that it's quite easy to confuse busy, engaged, compliant students and an organised, well-paced lesson with learning. While all of these things no doubt contribute to learning, they do not mean it is happening. One of the best ways to ensure that learning does occur is to identify, with absolute clarity, what that learning is and how it will be evidenced. Precisely articulated objectives are one of the best ways of achieving this.

This chapter focuses specifically on the use of objectives as a technique for framing the learning in lessons. Learning objectives are now ubiquitous in schools, but that doesn't mean that they are the only way to plan. You may be asked, as part of your academic study, to research alternative approaches in which the teacher doesn't determine the learning outcomes. The progressive education movement in the 1960s and 1970s advocated a child-centred approach, in which students were encouraged to discover the learning for themselves. A key proponent of such thinking was A. S. Neill, who believed that the imposition of learning, as opposed to the discovery, was the wrong approach (Neill, 1963). You might also refer to the work of Maria Montessori, whose ideas are still implemented in the worldwide Montessori school network (Montessori, 1998), or the somewhat eccentric ideas proposed by Rudolf Steiner (1996).

In this chapter, though, we will focus on the manner in which objectives are used to meet your learning and assessment goals in the classroom. In this respect, the use of objectives is essentially a behaviourist technique, in that it determines prescribed outcomes that amount to a change in behaviour. Through the use of objectives, you prime the students for the learning and they experience a sense of success if they can demonstrate the learning has been achieved. They act as a route map for classroom efficacy, especially if the process is transparent for all to see.

However, let's sound a cautionary note at this stage. It could be argued that a teacher might *limit* the learning if adherence to learning objectives becomes the *sole* focus of the lesson. Objectives are useful, but they are not exclusive. Any number of opportunities for additional learning might arise in a lesson. They might be the result of something a student asks, a conversation about something related that arises, or indeed just deeper analysis than the objectives anticipate. Staying alert to all learning opportunities is critically important in fostering an exploratory and curious learning culture in your classroom. With that caveat in place, let's look at how objectives work effectively.

REFLECTIVE QUESTION

- Should the learning be pre-determined in the lesson or should the teacher and students be seeking learning opportunities as the lesson progresses? Can both be achieved?

THE IMPORTANCE OF EFFECTIVE OBJECTIVES

Quality lessons are sharply focused on the learning. Identifying, with absolute clarity, what it is that we want our students to know, do or understand, right at the beginning of the planning process, can help us to ensure that we do this (while remembering to stay alert for additional opportunities). If we think of a lesson as an exposition, our overall intention is to use the time to convey, and more importantly to embed in students' long-term memory, knowledge, understanding, skills and/or thinking abilities. Objectives are the means by which we articulate this to students (and ourselves), making it clear exactly what is going to be learnt. They are, in essence, success criteria for the learning. They can also serve as inspiration for your students – it is very satisfying to embark on a goal-oriented process and then achieve it.

What we are aiming for is to introduce new knowledge, then allow the students to make use of this knowledge and, hopefully, engage them in some quality thinking in relation to it, because doing so embeds it. The objectives structure this process, supporting transfer from short-term to long-term memory, through recall, application and the use of thinking skills (more on this in Chapter 3). If the students are not thinking, they are not learning.

OBJECTIVES THAT ARTICULATE THE LEARNING

One of most common mistakes made is that the objectives are simply an articulation of the tasks that are going to be carried out in the lesson. Objectives of this sort might look like:

- We will use quadratic equations
- We will make use of commas when employing a subordinating conjunction
- We will calculate the angles in a triangle
- We will cover the function of the eye
- We will be aware of flashbacks in improvisation
- We will study the character of the Inspector
- We will familiarise ourselves with a product design

These objectives have learning implicit within them, but the key to really good objective writing is to ensure that *they are explicit in articulating the learning.* So, what might the objectives above look like if articulated as learning?

- We will know how to use quadratic equations
- We will understand where to use commas in relation to a subordinating conjunction
- We will know what the angles in a triangle should be
- We will understand the functioning of the eye
- We will learn how to use flashbacks in our improvisation
- We will explore the character of the Inspector
- We will make a good product design

All very well and good, but do they really get to the nub of the learning? Of equal importance, how do we assess them? How do we know what somebody else knows? In Chapter 7 on assessment, we look at assessment for learning, the core of which is being able to ascertain what the students have learnt. How do we measure accurately what somebody *understands or knows*? The verbs in Table 4.1 are extremely difficult to assess with any level of objectivity and are consequently best avoided.

Table 4.1   Cognitive events that are difficult to assess

Know	Understand	Realise	Be aware	Apprehend
Cover	Learn	Assimilate	Appreciate	Familiarise
Study	Explore	Comprehend	Recognise	Perceive

We need, therefore, to articulate the objectives in terms of the knowledge, skills and understanding we want to develop, while ensuring that we leave ourselves capacity to assess them objectively. If we are clear in our use of language, this can be achieved and will also build in some very clear success criteria for the students to work towards. The key to this is to use 'active verbs' rather than 'passive verbs', or, stated more plainly, ensure that the verb involves the student undertaking a specific action, providing opportunity for the learning to be demonstrated. The key benefit is that this is something you can then assess. For example:

- You will successfully *solve* a quadratic equation *using* factorisation
- You will *use* commas accurately to *construct* sentences containing subordinating conjunctions
- You will *explain* and *show your working* when *calculating* unknown angles within a triangle
- You will *identify* and *describe* the different elements of the function of the eye, then *design* a diagram illustrating this
- You will *apply* flashback to an improvisation, successfully *demonstrating* a change of time and place

- You will *analyse* and *explain* the role of the Inspector in conveying Priestley's intentions
- You will *describe, select* and *apply* design skills in *creating* a product

You may look at some of these and think they have not changed a great deal; it is in their specificity that the advantage is gained. Each of the third group of objectives ensures that the students know exactly what it is they should be able to do, remember or understand and also how this will be evidenced. The tasks are there, but the tasks are secondary to demonstrating the learning.

The active verbs marked in italics make the difference to these objectives. Quality objectives will always contain active verbs. If they are missing, the demonstrable learning probably is too. Table 4.2 provides some active verbs that will help you to formulate some objectives.

Table 4.2 Verbs that enable students to evidence their learning

Explain	Demonstrate	Analyse	Formulate	Discuss
Compare	Differentiate	Describe	Name	Assess
Evaluate	Identify	Design	Define	List
Express	Recall	Demonstrate	Employ	Conclude

THREE-TIER-THINKING: STRUCTURING AND SEQUENCING YOUR OBJECTIVES

Organising our objectives so that they sequence the learning for students is critical. If our objectives expect too much at the start of the lesson, or if they don't provide sufficient opportunity for the learning to be strengthened in the latter stages, they could be counterproductive. Our understanding of the role of knowledge is critical here.

REFLECTIVE QUESTION

- Which do you think is the most important type of learning? Gaining knowledge? The development of skills? The ability to think critically or creatively? See Gibb (2015), Hirsch (2016), Robinson (1998), and Claxton and Lucas (2010).

Knowledge has its place and it is the bedrock upon which success in the other areas is based (my view, others might argue otherwise). However, real intelligence, real skill and understanding come with the ability to apply that knowledge to analyse, evaluate and create.

All high-functioning roles, be it business entrepreneur, barrister, research scientist, film director, stockbroker, designer, musician or computer programmer, require this skill-set to be successful. The real joy of this is that these processes then feedback to the knowledge and understanding, deepening them also. Sequencing carefully helps us to achieve this.

Sequencing our objectives so that they effectively sequence the learning and use of knowledge is therefore a key skill for you to develop. The model we are going to use for setting objectives is called 'three-tier-thinking' (TTT). The model, as the title suggests, contains three stages (see Figure 4.1).

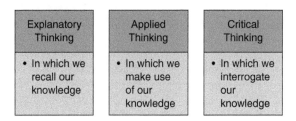

Figure 4.1   The three-tier-thinking model

Let's consider this in more detail. *Explanatory thinking, applied thinking* and *critical thinking* refers to that which we traditionally think of when we refer to knowledge. How much can we recall? We can't move to the next thinking stages if we can't remember the thing we are thinking about! We certainly won't pass an exam in English Literature if we can't access the information we need about the plotline in *Macbeth*, for example. Culturally, we set great store in people's ability to recall facts, figures, quotes and so on. This is one of the reasons why the current curriculum and assessment frameworks are constructed as they are. Interestingly, this ability is often conflated with intelligence. Arguably, the ability to remember information does not indicate that the person has great insight, creativity or understanding, it simply illustrates that they have a very effective long-term memory. Understanding knowledge is different from recalling it, which leads us to the next stage, *applied thinking*.

Understanding is different from knowledge in a very specific way. Knowledge is the information we need for understanding. Understanding is the way in which we make sense of that knowledge, through relating it to other pieces of knowledge, or to other specific contexts. This is where we start to apply the knowledge, and in doing so, deepen our understanding of its relevance, how it might be used elsewhere, and in so doing, we develop new knowledge.

An example of this might be that we have begun by recalling our times tables. Times tables also require us to recall that numbers have factors. Factors can also inform our understanding of fractions. In working out 1/7 of 49, we would use our 7 times table. Overall, both of these concepts illustrate that larger things can be broken down into parts of a similar size. We might then apply this understanding when understanding the concept of ratio, using both factors and fractions to inform how equal distribution works. In this example, we have applied knowledge to develop understanding and also strengthened, through recall, our access to existing knowledge.

Critical thinking is where we use our understanding, achieved through both recall and application, to really dig deep into knowledge and interrogate it. Arguably, this is where we really start to develop our intelligence. In order to interrogate, our understanding has to be strong and it also needs to be comprehensive. Critical thinking requires us to adopt a macro-view of knowledge, perceiving it from a variety of perspectives and understanding it in great depth. Critical thinking might also allow us to be able to invent new knowledge and understanding, as we step beyond the confines of knowledge that is already established. It engages us in finding reasons for things and research demonstrates that it is effective in strengthening learning (Coe et al., 2014).

An example of this might include writing an essay in which we explore the character of Juliet, interrogating how she is presented in the play by Shakespeare. To do so, we need to recall the plotline, her interactions with other characters and her key decisions. We also need to recall our knowledge of Shakespeare's context when the play was written. We then need to make decisions about why these things happen, using our knowledge of the text to evidence our judgements. An extension to this might be to write a scene that occurs if she decides not to fake her death, using our creativity, our knowledge of the whole text and our understanding of how characters might react. In both activities, our full knowledge is employed to develop deeper understanding and this knowledge has to be interrogated, dissected and reconstructed to create new meanings.

This model draws on a variety of sources to provide a framework that is both easy for you to recall and easy to apply. It is similar to a taxonomy, such as the work of Bloom (1956) or Biggs and Collins (1982). Taxonomies are classification systems. If you enjoy ordered and structured thinking, then they can be an incredibly useful tool in developing your practice, as they provide useful frameworks that enable you to think distinctively about different stages of your lessons. Bloom's Taxonomy articulates a range of different thinking modes that start with remembering and concludes with creating (for example, see Anderson & Krathwold, 2001).

The model also draws on cognitive theory, specifically as it pertains to memory. Models that illustrate the transfer from short-term to long-term memory emphasise the importance of application (Atkinson & Shiffrin, 1968). Put simply, students need to use the knowledge that they have acquired if they are going to recall it at later stages.

Rosenshine's (2010) ideas about sequencing also correlate to the TTT model. We explore Rosenshine in some detail in Chapter 3 on learning. His model describes a process in which the knowledge is introduced, checked and then applied.

There is a caveat to this. In the next section, we look at how the model can be used to articulate your objectives. This is done in a way that employs each of the thinking categories within a lesson. There is no need for you to do this, although there may be occasions when you choose to. The likelihood is that, in much the same way as Rosenshine recommends, you won't use each of the tiers in every lesson. Across a sequence of lessons, you may begin by focusing predominantly on explanatory thinking, whereas at later stages, you may be seeking to move your student to critical thinking as they have the knowledge they need to do this.

USING THE TTT MODEL TO IDENTIFY OBJECTIVES

What might objectives that employ the TTT model look like? If we take an example from a secondary English lesson in which the class are studying *An Inspector Calls*, the objectives could read something like this:

- We will *define* the following terms: Socialism, social class, capitalism. And then we will *identify* and *explain* what the Inspector says about social class.

This is obviously about knowledge and understanding. Students need to be able to find the key quotes and familiarise themselves with the content. They need to be able to use their knowledge of the play's themes to identify content that might pertain to class or social commentary.

The second objective would look to deepen this analysis, positioning the students more analytically, requiring them to apply this knowledge to foster further understanding and subsequently strengthen recall.

- We will identify relevant quotations and then use them to explain what the characters think about the key terms from objective 1.

Students are now explicitly engaged in analysis. They are also applying this analysis to deepen their knowledge of the text by exploring its meaning, as articulated by the characters.

The final objective might be task-specific, or might arise from the other work as an additional consideration. It will aim to enable the students to make use of their new macro-view of the Inspector's actions and interactions in developing their understanding of the meaning of the whole text: they are required to think critically.

- We will *explain and evaluate* the effectiveness of the play in conveying the socialist perspective.

Or you could create something task-specific, such as:

- We will write a letter to Mr Birling, from the Inspector, in which he outlines his concerns about the Birling family and explains why they represent what is wrong with Britain in 1912.

The implications for our planning are now clear: the lesson has to somehow centre on these objectives and you can see how the tasks that students undertake might arise from them. We are now engaged in objective-led planning.

KEEPING THE OBJECTIVES ALIVE

Now that we understand that we can focus our lesson from the outset, we need to ensure that our teaching, and subsequently the learning, remains focused on the direction that we have set. It's not enough to simply articulate the objectives and set the tasks – this is a key pitfall to avoid. There are many lessons in which the objectives are shared with the class at the outset and never mentioned again. We need to ensure that we structure the process of the lesson in a way that lends itself to objective completion and that means that they need to form part of the ongoing dialogue of the lesson.

There are some simple methods for this. A Religious Studies teacher from Hertfordshire invented a wonderfully simple way of keeping the objectives alive. She used PowerPoints for her lessons and on each slide she created a vertical column which sat at the edge of the screen, within which sat the objectives: a simple but effective reminder of what we are trying to achieve as we progress. This might go some way towards ensuring that the objectives are met.

We need to employ a little more sophistication if we are going to reach all of the students, though.

Returning to some of the previous objectives that we considered, let's look at the design example:

- Select and apply skills to design a product

This might be further broken down as follows:

- We will research and identify the materials and structure needed to create an efficient art easel. (explanatory thinking)
- We will analyse different models and select, with justification based on our research, the most effective design. (applied thinking)
- We will modify one area of the design to improve stability or aesthetic impact. (critical thinking)

As you can see, this progresses from knowledge and understanding, through to analysis and evaluation, culminating in creative application of both. The students might have different starting points.

The result of planning in this way is that the lesson has really structured itself. The students are aware, individually and based upon their individual starting points, what needs to be done and how they will demonstrate their progress, both to themselves and to you.

This then provides you with the opportunity to both check on and signal the learning at various stages of the lesson. In your planning, it may look something like Table 4.3.

Table 4.3   How activities arise from the objectives and how we check on learning

Task	Success criteria	Check on learning
Individually, create a list of materials needed to create an art easel.	A comprehensive list is identified and recorded.	Work scrutiny. Circulation and questioning. 'Class Objective Check' – who is meeting objective 1?
Individually, identify and describe the features of efficient art easels. As a group, modify lists according to consensus.	A list of useful features is correctly compiled and students are able to justify their choices.	Questioning following circulation – students to justify their lists. Use think–pair–share, but also target individuals whose lists were shorter or who identified unnecessary features.
Model a good design. Teacher to verbalise thinking. As a group, using a range of models, select an easel design.	Students make appropriate selections based on their knowledge of effective easel designs.	Classroom discussion. Students are able to articulate, through questioning, the features of effective easel designs. Circulation to check choices from the range – seek verbal justification for the choices and offer feedback.
Individually, provide a written justification for the selection.	Students are able to articulate the reasons for their selections, applying their knowledge from the lesson.	Students share their justifications with the group verbally. Interrogate these through targeted questioning. 'Class Objective Check' – who is meeting objective 2?

You can see that the activities effectively cascade from the objectives. You will also note that the teacher has identified where and how they will check on the learning, as well as the specific things that they will be looking for. In this manner, the objectives become an embedded part of the lesson. The 'Class Objective Check' feature is effectively a mini-plenary in which the teacher is engaging the students in reflection on their own progress against the objectives, developing their metacognition. The teacher at this stage has done this themselves at various stages through work scrutiny, questioning and classroom discussion.

QUESTIONING AND OBJECTIVES

Really good teachers use questions effectively. They use them: to manage the classroom; to focus an individual student on the task; to challenge an assumption; to posit a problem; to add humour; to build a relationship; to create tension; to deceive; to be controversial; to stretch and challenge; to foster debate; to check understanding; to assess; to influence; to flatter – we could go on. It is a skilful business and warrants a book of its own.

We are going to look specifically at how questions can be used to generate learning related to the objectives. Some of this will be incidental in the sense that opportunities to explore an idea or concept invariably arise in the lesson, usually as the result of student questions. These should not be ignored, but they are difficult to anticipate and therefore present a difficulty in terms of planning.

The aim here is to align our questioning to our planning and our stated objectives. Let's look at our science example – the functioning of the eye. Let's begin by articulating our objectives, using the three-tier structure that we have just discussed. The objectives might look something like this:

- Accurately label a diagram that illustrates the components of the eye and explain the function of the iris and the sclera. (explanatory thinking)
- Explain, using findings from experiments and key vocabulary, depth perception and the student reflex. (applied thinking)
- Select, based on your knowledge of functionality, the correct lens for modification of a long-sighted eye. (explanatory and critical thinking)

Questions in this lesson will be planned in advance and might be structured as follows:

OBJECTIVE 1

- Can you name the key elements of the eye?
- Can you locate the iris?
- The cornea is in the centre of the eye – true or false?
- Who can describe what can be found at the rear of the pupil?

These questions are simple enough and only require students to provide an accurate summary of the key facts that they have learnt. The process of checking these answers has the function of consolidating learning.

OBJECTIVE 2

- What do you think would happen if the sclera was not present or suddenly disappeared?
- Why is the pupil reflex a useful function of the eye?
- Is your perception of depth better with monocular or binocular vision?
- Who can give me a concise definition of the pupil reflex?
- Why do carnivores have eyes at the front of their heads?

These questions require the students to apply their knowledge and begin to explain the functionality in more experiential terms. They engage the students in speculation based on what they have just learnt and prepare them for understanding of the eye in totality.

OBJECTIVE 3

- Why, when objects are near, might the lens need to be thicker?
- Compare and identify two differences in the cause and effect of vision problems?
- Look at this diagram of a lens and an eye with vision problems. What changes would you recommend to the optician?
- Compare these two lenses: which would be more effective for treating a short-sighted person?

These questions require higher order, interrogative thinking. Students need to make sense of previous knowledge, apply their understanding of the overall functionality of the eye and then evaluate the impact of different conditions based upon this.

Planning our questions in advance does not take very long and ensures that we are both scaffolding, drawing out and stretching the learning as we progress through the lesson. Linking them tightly to the objectives ensures that we remain focused on the outcomes we want for the students. Table 4.4 shows some questions stems that you might employ to develop your questioning, using the three-tier-thinking model.

Table 4.4 Three-tier-thinking question stems

Explanatory thinking		
Can you list...?	Which one...?	Can you locate...?
Can you recall...?	How would you classify...?	How would you define...?
How do you...?	Which approach would...?	Who can remember...?
How would you show...?	What is the idea behind...?	Using your own words,
When did...?	Which statements support...?	can you...?
Where is...?	Who could teach us...?	Which statements illustrate...?
What is...?	Who can find...?	How would you summarise...?
Applied thinking		
How would you use...?	What inference can you	Choose the elements
Can you solve...?	make...?	that would...?
What's the relationship	What do you think...?	Hypothesise how...?
between... and...?	Suppose you could...?	How could you change...?
Which is the most/least...?	Can you predict...?	Could we copy...?
What approach would...?	How would you organise...?	What happens if...?
Identify the difference/similarity	What could we do if...?	Imagine if...?
between... and...?	How would you classify...?	What stages would be
What do you notice...?	How else might we...?	needed to...?
Critical thinking		
Do you agree with...?	What's wrong with...?	Which would you choose to...?
How would you improve...?	Why is...?	Would you recommend...?
Can you suggest an	Which would you prioritise...?	Convince me that...?
alternative...?	What is the value of...?	How might we oppose...?
How would you test...?	How would you justify...?	What's brilliant about...?
What would you estimate...?	Which is best for...?	Why did they...?

DEVELOPING CLASSROOM TALK

Being able to pose questions, and receive answers, is a skill that you will develop over time. As you become more proficient in generating classroom talk through your use of questions, you can look to develop your competence in using classroom oracy to deepen the learning, meet your objectives and ensure that your clearly articulated success criteria have been met. Wragg and Brown's (2001) research demonstrated that questions and classroom talk consolidate learning, strengthen recall and also allow for checking of understanding, particularly when those questions are related to the objectives of the lesson.

Effective classroom talk contributes to an effective culture of learning, as well as providing you with an opportunity to carry out checks on learning in a time-efficient manner. You may find that encouraging students to answer your questions is problematic at first, but there are some ways in which you can develop this quickly.

Sherrington (2021) states that Lemov's (2010) cold-calling is the number 1 technique for classroom inclusion. Essentially, this means no-hands-up. Ask the class a question (for examples, see above), give them some thinking time, and then identify an individual to whom you wish to direct it. Listen to their answer and offer your response, then ask another student to respond. They might respond to the first student's answer, or they may respond to the original question, depending on the outcomes. If you're systematic and strategic about whom you ask and when, it's possible to ensure that everybody has made verbal contributions in the lesson.

Another way of ensuring responses is to use methods that foster confidence. Students will often be reluctant to speak if they are uncertain about what they are saying – nobody likes to get it wrong in public. Create shared ownership and diffuse that tension by using think–pair–share. In this strategy, you pose the question. Students then consider their responses in pairs, and in so doing consolidate their understanding together. They also take shared ownership of the answers, which acts as a buffer to issues with confident response. You can then cold-call the pairs to gauge their responses.

How you respond when students offer answers is also critical in developing both confidence and the culture that you want to encourage. Be supportive and encouraging. If a student is unable to answer, don't humiliate them with responses like, 'You should know that'. If a student gets it wrong or provides a ridiculous answer, don't let laughter from other students go unchallenged. If you can see that they are really struggling and becoming uncomfortable, don't keep pressing – ask somebody else to help them out.

One key element to consider are the types of responses that you want from students – these are dependent on the questions that you ask. Some questions require a very specific response in that there may be only one correct answer. We can think of these questions as deductive. Inductive questions are the opposite of this and require the respondent to speculate, hypothesise, infer, generalise. There is room for both types of questions across the curriculum, with inductive questions likely to be employed at the top end of the three-tier-thinking model.

Robin Alexander, a professor at the University of Cambridge, is an expert in classroom talk and focuses sharply on *dialogic* teaching techniques (Alexander, 2020). This builds on the ideas introduced above and is a process in which, through classroom talk, students build on each other's ideas and deepen learning as a result. There are a set of key skills and questioning types that teachers can develop to support this process. The Education Endowment Foundation (2017) commissioned a report that found these strategies can foster additional progress to the tune of two additional months in science and English, and one month in maths (across two academic terms).

Alexander (2020) outlines a process in which instead of just using explanation and instruction (followed by deductive questions and responses), teacher talk is extended to also foster debate and dialogue (through inductive questioning and responses). Wrong answers don't matter; there are none in truth, as they simply open up more debate. In such classroom talk, students are invited to test ideas, tackle problems, speculate, offer extended answers, consider alternative viewpoints, build on each other's answers, problematise and generally prise open their capacity for divergent thinking (exploring multiple explanations).

STRATEGIES FOR SUCCESS

This is the section in which we look at how you might make use of information to support your teaching. Following that, we consider some additional strategies that support the focus of this chapter.

GATHER YOUR INFORMATION

Ensuring that individual students meet their objectives necessitates a good understanding of each student's potential in relation to those objectives. How likely is each individual in the room to achieve your learning intentions? What does their prior progress and attainment suggest about this likelihood?

Keeping a record of your students' progress in lessons will help you to answer these questions effectively. This may amount to more than spreadsheets of assessment scores. Keep a record of their strengths; the sessions when they made a progress leap (work out why that happened); the sessions when they appeared to really struggle (again, why); the types of activities that seem to really suit them and the types that don't; and the particular topic areas that seem to present a challenge or seem to be an area of strength.

In addition, you might want to gather information from across the curriculum. Gain access to their full academic reports and see how they are achieving in other lessons or in historical years. Perhaps they did really well in Year 4 in Humanities, but in Year 5 they are not sufficiently making progress in related subjects? What could be the cause of this and what are the implications for your objectives and the strategies required to meet them? They seem to be doing really well in maths in Year 11, but their physics grade is much higher – why? Use this information to have professional conversations with fellow teachers: are you structuring your objectives (and subsequently your tasks) in a manner that is hindering progress?

Most importantly, create a strategy, possibly over a sequence of lessons, that enables you to have one-to-one conversations with students in a manner that supports your understanding of how they learn, the level of their understanding and their learning obstacles. Many teachers find it difficult to do this within the time constraints the profession creates, but it is critically important, so make time to give it some explicit thought. There is no substitute for this, but it can be supplemented through marking, Assessment for Learning processes and through questioning. Build a picture: know your students.

REFLECTION AFTER THE LESSON

- Did the students achieve the objectives?
- How many of them did I observe evidencing the intended learning?
- Did my objectives articulate learning or tasks?
- Were the students able to articulate their learning at the end of the lesson?
- Which students struggled with the objectives?
- Do those struggles have implications for differentiation moving forward?
- Was I able to assess the learning as I had anticipated?
- Did the objectives support each other or was I trying to squeeze too much in?
- Was there sufficient challenge built in for students at all levels?

TIPS FOR EFFECTIVE USE OF OBJECTIVES

ACTIVE VERBS

- Make sure that your objectives contain verbs that allow students to demonstrate their learning.

(Continued)

ASSESS THROUGH YOUR OBJECTIVES

- Phrase your objectives so that they provide you with something tangible to assess.

USE ATTAINMENT DATA

- Ensure that your objectives are informed by attainment and progress data – where do they need to focus their effort?

USE FINDINGS FROM PLENARIES

- Record your findings from plenary discussions and use them to identify objectives for future lessons.

USE SYLLABUS MATERIALS

- If teaching an examination syllabus, use the assessment objectives and support resources from examination board websites to inform your objectives.

USE TTT FOR STRUCTURE

- Explanatory thinking – Applied thinking – Critical thinking. Use this as a loose framework for deepening understanding in the lesson, assisting the transfer from short-term to long-term memory.

USE TTT FOR QUESTIONS

- Plan your questions to both augment and assess progress towards the objectives, using the taxonomy as a guide.

TARGET YOUR QUESTIONS CAREFULLY TO GAUGE INDIVIDUAL LEARNING AND TO FOSTER DEEPER UNDERSTANDING

- Develop a strategy that enables you to speak to all students over time – the more frequently, the better.

KEEP THE OBJECTIVES ALIVE

- Don't just read them out at the beginning. Refer to them, include them in resources, plan questions around them, evaluate them.

USE CLASSROOM TALK TO GAUGE STUDENTS SUCCESS IN MEETING THE OBJECTIVES

- Look to develop inductive talk and dialogic teaching, both of which are a sophisticated means of consolidating and extending the learning articulated in your objectives.

SUMMARY

In this chapter, we have covered:

- Objectives should be thought of as success criteria for your lesson. Articulate them carefully so that they structure the learning and the means by which you will assess it.
- Plan your lessons so that the objectives remain active throughout the learning. Speak to pupils about them frequently and engage them in assessing their own progress against them.
- Three-tier-thinking is a useful tool for structuring your objectives so that they strengthen commitment to long-term memory and subsequent recall.
- Classroom talk has a significant role to play in learning. This can be approached with different levels of sophistication. Building a culture in which students engage freely in deep levels of dialogue, related to your objectives, is likely to strengthen learning.

REFERENCES

Alexander, J. (2020) *A Dialogic Teaching Companion.* London: Routledge.

Anderson, L. W., & Krathwohl, D. R. (2001) *A Taxonomy for Learning, Teaching and Assessing: A Revision of Bloom's Taxonomy of Educational Objectives.* Complete Edition. New York: Longman Bloom.

Atkinson, R. C., & Shiffrin, R. M. (1968) Human memory: A proposed system and its control processes. In K. W. Spence & J. T. Spence (eds), *The Psychology of Learning and Motivation* (Volume *2*, pp. 89–195). New York: Academic Press.

Biggs, J., & Collis, K. (1982) *Evaluating the Quality of Learning: The SOLO Taxonomy*. New York: Academic Press.

Bloom, B. S. (1956) *Taxonomy of Educational Objectives*, Handbook: The Cognitive Domain. David McKay, New York.

Claxton, G., & Lucas, B. (2010) *New Kinds of Smart: How the Science of Learnable Intelligence is Changing Education*. London: Open University Press.

Coe, R., Aloisis, C., Higgin, S., & Elliot-Major, L. (2014) *What Makes Great Teaching? A Review of the Underpinning Research*. London: Sutton Trust.

Education Endowment Foundation (2017) *Dialogic Teaching: Evaluation Report and Executive Summary*. London: EEF. Accessed online (13 July 2021) at: https://educationendowmentfoundation.org.uk/public/files/Projects/Evaluation_Reports/Dialogic_Teaching_Evaluation_Report.pdf

Gibb, N. (2015) *The Social Justice Case for an Academic Curriculum*. Accessed online (10 September 2018) at: www.gov.uk/government/speeches/nick-gibb-the-social-justice-case-for-an-academic-curriculum

Hirsch, E. D. (2016) *Why Knowledge Matters: Rescuing Our Children from Failed Educational Theories*. Cambridge, MA: Harvard University Press.

Lemov, D. (2010) *Teach like a Champion*. San Francisco, CA: Jossey-Bass.

Montessori, M. (1998) *The Montessori Method*. New York: Schocken Books.

Neill, A. S. (1963) *Summerhill: A Radical Approach to Child Rearing*. Oxford: Hart Publishing.

Robinson, K. (1998) *All Our Futures: Creativity, Culture and Education*. London: Department for Education and Employment.

Rosenshine, B. (2010) *Principles of Instruction*. The International Academy of Education (IAE) *Educational Practices* Series 21. London: IAE.

Sherrington, T. (2021) Cold Calling: The #1 strategy for inclusive classrooms – remote and in person. *teacherhead* [Blog]. Posted 7 February 2021. Accessed online (13 July 2021) at: https://teacherhead.com/2021/02/07/cold-calling-the-1-strategy-for-inclusive-classrooms-remote-and-in-person/

Steiner, R. (1996) *The Education of the Child*. Hudson, NY: Anthroposophic Press.

Wragg, E. C., & Brown, G. A. (2001) *Questioning in the Primary School*. London: Routledge.

5

OBSTACLES TO LEARNING

IN THIS CHAPTER, WE WILL COVER:

- What obstacles to learning might a student experience
- How do these obstacles manifest in the classroom
- What are the statutory duties in relation to these obstacles
- What support can be offered to students with obstacles

INTRODUCTION

The aim of this chapter is to provide an overview of some of the obstacles to learning that might be experienced by students. This is a complex area, and one that is riddled with misconceptions. Those misconceptions can lead to a host of well-intentioned, but sometimes counterproductive efforts on the part of both teachers and schools.

The potential range and nature of these obstacles is well beyond the scope of a single chapter in this book. What we can do is focus on some of the most prevalent examples and look at some of the ways in which you might mitigate and/or support students.

The fact is that we all experience obstacles in our learning. One of the best ways to understand this is through a memory exercise.

To help you along with this exercise, bear with me as I recount one of my own. I attended a training session, relatively early in the days of personal computing, in which the aim was to be able to use spreadsheets effectively. One of our tasks was to create a table that contained some formulas. I was in a room full of other teachers, varying in levels of experience. The session was led by our charismatic, inspirational, but slightly impatient deputy head (who loved a spreadsheet).

As soon as the task was set, I made my first attempt, then froze: I couldn't do it. For some reason, the sequential nature of his verbal instructions eluded me. Some old ghosts began to waft through me: maths inadequacy raised its head and I began to recall secondary maths lessons in the 1980s – the silence, the austere monitoring of our imposing teacher, the inability to complete and the need to hide. I looked around the room and quickly surmised that everybody else was managing perfectly well. Formulas were popping up on screens everywhere and people looked so happy and content, sharing their success with each other amiably. Their success looked so easy.

You will not be surprised to learn that, rather than ask for help, I pretended to create formulas. My embarrassment was acute. I couldn't be seen not to understand. I couldn't ask the deputy. I was picturing his exasperation and fully expected scorn and disdain if I asked again – he'd already explained it and everybody else was managing, so why couldn't I? I managed to dissemble my way through the whole session. On the way out, I chatted with my colleagues about how well it had all gone and how formulas were much easier than expected and that I would definitely be using them henceforth. Ridiculous, I know – why not just speak up?

REFLECTIVE QUESTIONS

- Have you ever experienced difficulty in accessing learning?
- How did this feel?
- What adaptations would have made this easier for you?

If we consider this scenario, and you think about your own experiences of being unable to 'keep up', it helps us to understand what it must feel like for those who experience this frequently. Learning in school is a social activity. Being unable to do 'the work' is a high visibility experience. 'Pretend work', as a student once explained to me, is one of many coping strategies employed by young people as they seek to maintain their social status within the complexity of school life. This is not the same as saying that every child who experiences an obstacle is going to react in this way – many of them cope with the situation much more effectively than I did – but it is worth remembering that struggling to achieve while many others around you succeed, because of circumstances beyond your control, is an emotional experience.

The key lesson we learn from this as teachers is the importance of empathy. If we seek to understand the obstacle itself and the strategies that might mitigate for it, then it stands to reason that we must also understand the emotional nuance that accompanies it. This implies patience, compassion, a willingness to go the extra mile, tenacity and resilience from teachers in not giving up and a sensitivity to the individual student and their lived experience within the context of the lesson.

Other sections of this book are pertinent here. In the section on differentiation in Chapter 6, we cover the importance of adapting for potential, not ability. The content of that chapter will also feed into the message of this one. An obstacle to learning is a challenge to be overcome; a student with such an obstacle is potential waiting to be released, and the effectiveness of really great teachers is linked indelibly to working in this way.

In this chapter, we consider the concept of obstacles quite broadly and focus on some of those that arise most frequently. This is accompanied by a look at some of the ways in which you might support students in whom these obstacles present. We consider the Autistic Spectrum and its impact, both socially and as a learner. We look at some specific learning difficulties, such as dyslexia and dyscalculia. Social and emotional difficulties, such as attention deficit (ADD) and anxiety, are covered. We also hone in on disadvantage, considering the impact on both school policy and the perception of teaching staff.

This chapter also comes with a caveat. The most we can hope to achieve here is the briefest of introductions. Please take the time to understand these obstacles and, more importantly, the children for whom they present. Take the time to do so during your training and as you progress further in your career. This is a moral imperative. If we are truly to improve our education system, this will be one of the key indicators that we have done so. Such an enterprise starts with you – the trainee teacher. Your potential for future influence is limitless.

STATUTORY DUTIES AND ACCOUNTABILITY FRAMEWORKS

In this section, we will look at the frameworks that determine provision for students with special educational needs (SEN) and the responsibilities that arise for schools and teachers.

SPECIAL EDUCATIONAL NEEDS AND DISABILITIES

The Children and Families Act 2014 is the key piece of legislation outlining the responsibilities of schools and local authorities in relation to students with Special Educational
Needs or Disabilities (SEND). The coverage extends to young people from birth until
the age of 25, as long as they remain in education or training. The local authority (LA)
has a duty to identify students whose needs might be supported by the provision of an
Education, Health and Care Plan (EHCP). Once a need or needs have been identified, the
plan articulates the support that should be provided. The school has a responsibility to
implement this plan, but it is the role of the LA to ensure that it is in place.

In England, the *SEN and Disability Code of Practice 0 to 25 Years* (Department for
Education, 2015) outlines the duties of schools and colleges. It articulates a process of
graduated support that culminates in, if judged to be necessary, an EHCP. The process
starts with careful monitoring and assessment of all students. If a student is identified as
requiring further support, schools are required to begin a cycle that involves teachers, the
student and the parents in ascertaining what that support would look like. As a teacher,
you will have a key role in such a process. Many of these initial processes begin in primary
school as students embark on their learning journeys, but it can be the case that SEN
may not be identified until secondary level. All teachers, therefore, whatever phase they
teach in, are required to maintain monitoring and assessment of all students. The cycle is
arranged in four parts (see Figure 5.1).

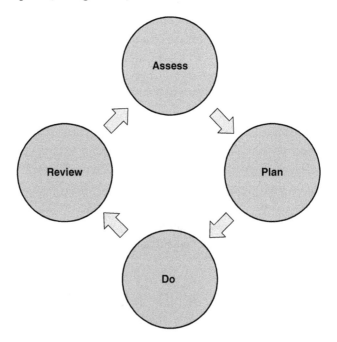

Figure 5.1   The graduated approach to SEND

Once this cycle is implemented in relation to an identified need, it becomes 'SEN Provision'. A graduated approach may then be implemented in which the cycle is run repeatedly, as understanding of the need and resulting support are developed. Dependent on the resulting progress made by the student, it may become necessary, as part of the review cycle, to involve external specialists in an assessment of the needs arising. At this point, a plan may be established and will involve parents/guardians, the school, the Special Educational Needs Coordinator (SENDCO) and external specialists. The plan will have some clearly identified outcomes for the student and a date for review. If the student continues to progress more slowly, at this point either the school or the parents (or both) might make the decision to request an EHCP.

Disability may form a part of these considerations. When this is the case, the Equality Act 2010 also features in shaping duties and expectations. This Act is concerned with preventing discrimination and increasing access; it also places duties on schools and LAs. Disability, for the purposes of definition, means:

> He or she has a physical or mental impairment and the impairment has a substantial and long-term adverse effect on his or her ability to carry out normal day-to-day activities. (Equality Act 2010, Part 1)

It is important to note here that we shouldn't conflate special educational needs and disability: one can exist without the other. However, they do present together for numbers of students. Due to changes in the law, students with disabilities now have increased rights to access education in mainstream settings, and consequently, schools and LAs have a duty to make the adjustments necessary to facilitate this.

DISADVANTAGED STUDENTS AND LEGISLATION

The Pupil Premium, introduced in 2012 by the then Coalition government, is designed to raise the achievement of disadvantaged students. The premium is an amount of money given directly to schools, with the money being allocated based on the number of disadvantaged students in the school. At the time of writing, this amounts to £1,345 per primary student and £955 per secondary student (Department for Education, 2021).

Eligibility for the funding is based on the following criteria:

- Receipt of the Ever6 free school meals programme, where students currently receive, or have received within the preceding six years, free school meals. Children adopted from care or who have left care (£2,345).
- Looked-after children (£2,345).

Schools are free to allocate the funds as they wish. This means that the money is not 'ring-fenced', a term that basically means a specific focus for spending. As a result, schools do not have to spend the money on the individual child. This means that much of the funding can be absorbed into cash-strapped school budgets.

However, there is a specific accountability structure built around disadvantaged students. First, schools must report, as a statutory duty, how the money has been spent, the impact on the disadvantaged students, and how they intend to spend the money in the following year.

The outcomes for disadvantaged students are reported on the government's school performance tables website and the Ofsted Inspection Handbook makes specific mention of their achievement in numerous places. Therefore, disadvantaged students and their achievement are a key focus for school leaders, and consequently, teaching staff. We will look at how that impacts on your practice later in the chapter.

Some might argue that there is no place for this group of students in a chapter on obstacles to learning. However, this issue is placed here for specific reasons related to some of those objections, which we will cover later in the chapter.

YOUR RESPONSIBILITY

The responsibilities for teachers to meet the needs of all students is articulated clearly in both the *Teachers' Standards* (Department for Education, 2011) and is a key component of the *Core Content Framework* for Initial Teacher Training (Department for Education, 2019). Teachers' Standard 5 states:

> 5. Adapt teaching to respond to the strengths and needs of all students.
>
> - know when and how to differentiate appropriately, using approaches which enable students to be taught effectively
> - have a secure understanding of how a range of factors can inhibit students' ability to learn, and how best to overcome these
> - demonstrate an awareness of the physical, social and intellectual development of children, and know how to adapt teaching to support students' education at different stages of development
> - have a clear understanding of the needs of all students, including those with special educational needs; those of high ability; those with English as an additional language; those with disabilities; and be able to use and evaluate distinctive teaching approaches to engage and support them. (Department for Education, 2011)

The *Core Content Framework* outlines a key number of areas of knowledge in relation to this standard that trainee teachers are expected to demonstrate they have acquired. The most pertinent to this chapter are outlined below:

> - Students are likely to learn at different rates and to require different levels and types of support from teachers to succeed.

- Seeking to understand students' differences, including their different levels of prior knowledge and potential barriers to learning, is an essential part of teaching.
- Adapting teaching in a responsive way, including by providing targeted support to students who are struggling, is likely to increase student success.
- Adaptive teaching is less likely to be valuable if it causes the teacher to artificially create distinct tasks for different groups of students or to set lower expectations for particular students.
- Students with special educational needs or disabilities are likely to require additional or adapted support; working closely with colleagues, families and students to understand barriers and identify effective strategies is essential. (Department for Education, 2019: 20)

As we have seen previously, a sound working knowledge of the *Core Content Framework* is essential to progressing effectively on a teacher training programme.

REFLECTIVE QUESTION

- Consider the *Core Content Framework* statements above. What relationship can you establish between these and our three guiding principles?

OBSTACLES EXPERIENCED BY STUDENTS

In this section, we will look at the four specific areas of need, focusing in on some specific conditions, and consider how you might support students in addressing these needs. We will consider how to work in a manner which is simultaneously inclusive and supportive. Finally, we will consider how disadvantage might impact on learning.

The four areas identified in the *SEN and Disability Code of Practice* (Department for Education, 2015) (Figure 5.2) are:

- Communication and interaction
- Cognition and learning
- Social, emotional and mental health
- Sensory and/or physical needs

If you look at Figure 5.2, it shows, as with most categorisations contained in this book, that it is not the intention to imply that these are mutually exclusive. There will be crossover: students may experience difficulty in more than one of these areas, a small number may experience a complex interacting range of difficulties, and some students' obstacles will be limited to one specific area. This is reflected in the structure of the following areas

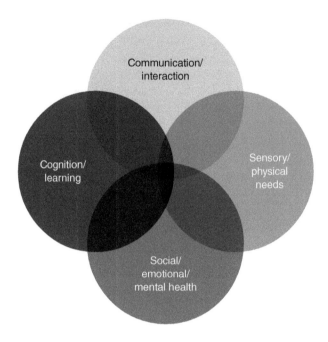

Figure 5.2 Four areas of need identified in the *SEN and Disability Code of Practice* (Department for Education, 2015)

of guidance. Additionally, the coverage here is far from exhaustive and you would be well advised to look at some specialist texts focusing on SEND to gain a broader overview.

COMMUNICATION AND INTERACTION

In this section, we will look at the role of communication in learning and the obstacles that students might experience in relation to this.

LANGUAGE IMPAIRMENT

Vygotsky (1962) argued that our ability to think is determined by our language. If we accept this to be the case, we can begin to realise the impact that difficulties with language are going to have on our capacity for learning. Communication, of course, is not solely reliant on language; we also have body language, eye contact, gesture and facial expression. But many of you will have experienced the limitations arising from making yourself understood using just these in a foreign country, or at a noisy concert, for example.

Students may experience language impairment ranging from an inability to use spoken language due to a disability or specific cognitive limitation, through to having a limited vocabulary or simply being new to the English language (English as an additional language, EAL). The difficulty may manifest receptively (understanding what is said/written) or expressively (coherent communication through speech or writing), or both.

REFLECTIVE QUESTION

- Consider the impact of language impairment in a mainstream classroom. What issues might arise for a student learning maths? Think about the implications arising from this for your own subject or phase.

In pronounced cases, specialists may use systems such as Alternative and Augmentative Communication (AAC), in which speech is replaced with other tools, such as pictograms or specific software. Teachers supporting students with needs such as these may receive specialist training and/or support to assist classroom practice.

However, your teaching can easily be pitched to support language acquisition, development and social use, through a focus on developing oral skills in social contexts. Try problem-solving aloud, use of drama and role-play, student explanations, dialogic teaching, students repeating instructions aloud, using think–pair–share, interviews, presentations, group work and socially-driven projects. Language development and interaction can also be supported through multi-sensory teaching in which meaning is communicated through various media/formats.

AUTISTIC SPECTRUM DISORDERS

Autism is not contained in this particular section because it is limited to cognition and learning. Young people with an Autistic Spectrum Disorder (ASD) may experience obstacles that manifest across all four areas in the *SEN and Disability Code of Practice* (Department for Education, 2015).

Wing and Gould (1979) are credited with a useful definition that can be categorised in three ways. The first is that autistic children may experience difficulty in social interaction and social relationships, such as recognising the feelings of others, following social rules, touch, or might display apparent indifference or insensitivity. The second is that they may experience difficulty with understanding communication, including, and sometimes specifically, non-verbal signals, such as facial expressions, body language or gesture. The third area they defined as 'social imagination'. This could include behaving in obsessive, restricted or repetitive ways. They might struggle to understand how others feel or the reasons for their actions. They might also find it difficult to appreciate concepts such as danger or risk.

In the classroom, children with ASD can be supported by the teacher with some effective planning and modifications.

- Keep things predictable and aim to reduce anything that might lead to additional distraction.
- Make sure that signals for quiet and/or gaining attention are both explicit and rehearsed.
- Create an area where sensory input can be reduced to a minimum – you might also provide headphones.
- Teach the language of emotion and find opportunities to relate emotion directly to experience.
- Work in a structured and explicit manner at all stages of the learning process.

COGNITION AND LEARNING

MODERATE LEARNING DIFFICULTIES

Students with moderate learning difficulties are likely to need adaption and additional support. Most learning that takes place in school involves the use of symbols; these symbols are used to represent ideas. Examples of this include letters to represent phonemes (the smallest units of sound in a word), the use of numbers, sound–symbol correspondence and so on. Abstract symbols, in order to be employed usefully, also require some understanding of the concepts that underpin them.

Moderate learning difficulties might mean that a student experiences difficulty making or sustaining these links. The challenge is to enable them to move from physical to abstract representation. They might be supported by 'doing' first through using manipulatives, or by being given additional time or through the support of visual aids. Scaffolding is also likely to have a role to play here; see the discussion on differentiation in Chapter 6 to understand how this method works, but essentially this is providing support and then withdrawing the support at appropriate points, eventually leading to independence. Cognitive science approaches are also worth trying. You might try 'chunking' the material, using a mastery approach in which success is secured before moving to the next level (see Chapter 3 on learning for more detail). Both Piaget (1964) and Bruner (1966) shed some light on this technique. Piaget identified the 'formal operational stage' and Bruner the 'symbolic representational stage', both of which constitute the latter stages of a child's ability to work in this manner.

REFLECTIVE QUESTION

- Look up Piaget's 'formal operational stage' and consider the implications for adaptive teaching. How might his research inform your practice?

SPECIFIC LEARNING DIFFICULTIES

Specific Learning Difficulties (SpLD) include dyslexia, dyspraxia, dyscalculia and dysgraphia. We will focus on dyslexia and dyscalculia, but please do take the time to do some reading on the others. Attention Deficit Disorder (ADD) is also considered a SpLD, but we will look at that in the section on social and emotional difficulties.

DYSLEXIA

Dyslexia is often mistaken, particularly in the early stages of education, as an issue with overall cognition. However, teachers should be aware that dyslexia is not indicative of other cognitive difficulties. As we have seen earlier, given that the curriculum is delivered within the text, it is no surprise that dyslexic students might appear to be slower to learn than their peers. However, this is for a very specific reason: difficulty with phonic decoding, hence the SpLD labelling. Phonic decoding is the process of translating symbol to sound, or grapheme to phoneme, which can impact in numerous ways.

Rose et al. (2009) provide us with a useful definition of dyslexia. They identify a number of effects that may arise from the condition, including: issues with reading and spelling, phonological awareness, verbal memory, verbal processing speed and language. Motor coordination, mental calculation, concentration and personal organisation might also be affected, but it is worth pointing out that features in this latter list do not in themselves constitute indicators of dyslexia.

Supporting students with dyslexia is a process requiring two specific strands. The first is to 'train' the student to recognise and overcome the difficulties as they present; the second is to support the student in being able to cope while building engagement and motivation around literacy. The latter is just as important. Training them to recognise and overcome the issues presenting might involve:

- Phonological awareness training
- Making up nonsense rhymes
- Various paired reading arrangements (reading out loud together, reading to each other, using recordings while tracking the text)
- Transcribing thoughts recorded on a phone/tablet to develop writing

- Being a scribe for the student
- Use of writing frames
- Multi-sensory teaching resources, diagrams, manipulatives, pictures, sound materials
- Use of screen filters on computers
- Use of coloured acetates when reading
- Over-learning (repetition of already learnt material)
- Use of mnemonics
- Give extra time
- Print on different-coloured paper

DYSCALCULIA

Up to 60% of students who experience difficulty with dyslexia can experience similar issues with mathematical ideas and operations (Miles &Miles, 2004). This can involve computational skills and mathematical reasoning. The issues that underpin dyslexia are likely to be similar to those that underpin dyscalculia.

Students may experience difficulty in a number of mathematically-specific areas. One of the key areas of difficulty is memory. A student with dyscalculia may struggle to remember times tables and division facts. They may also struggle with multi-step questions or calculations with several stages, or with sequencing, such as months in the year. In addition, they may experience difficulty with orientation, such as left/right distinctions, or writing in columns and working in rows. This can extend to making sense of visual information, such as bar charts, graphs, coordinates, angles and so on.

You might support them by:

- Using multi-sensory strategies (handling while verbalising)
- Chanting and rhythmic repetition
- Recall exercises, such as remembering groups of objects
- Collaborative learning
- Talking through problems before attempting them
- Use of manipulatives
- Visual representations such as number lines
- Cuisenaire Rods
- Reducing pressure and allowing time
- Focusing on building confidence and engagement

SOCIAL, EMOTIONAL AND MENTAL HEALTH

Thankfully, issues such as these are now part of a meaningful dialogue about how to support young people through their education. All of us, at some point in our lives, are likely to experience difficulty in one or more of these areas. Part of learning to be an effective teacher is about learning to form respectful, trusting relationships with students, irrespective of their background. If you manage to do this, the likelihood of a student feeling comfortable about disclosing a difficulty to you is higher. Even if you are not part of the disclosure process, you will be part of the support network. Sometimes your involvement in support may be specific and explicit, and on other occasions, you may not be made aware of the difficulties a student is going through, at which point, the manner in which you conduct yourself and interact with students generally can either become part of the difficulty or part of the support. The key to doing this well is to ensure that, as we discuss in Chapter 8 in the section on student behaviour, you look past the behaviours themselves and ask yourself questions about what might be the underlying causes.

There are a huge range of social and emotional and mental health issues. We can't cover them all in the space afforded here, so we will focus on some of the more common ones.

ATTENTION DEFICIT AND HYPERACTIVITY DISORDER (ADHD)

ADHD is a neurodevelopmental condition. Conditions of this sort can affect memory, behaviour, self-regulation, concentration and capacity for learning. Students with ADHD may struggle to remain still, struggle with impulse-control, struggle to follow directions and instructions, become easily distracted, talk at inappropriate times and interrupt. Some students may not present the hyperactive elements of the condition and are sometimes referred to as having ADD. Students with ADHD may also experience difficulty with meta-cognition and executive functioning, which can affect time-management, organisation and prioritisation. They may also struggle with sleep, which can exacerbate the problems they are experiencing.

Students experiencing ADHD *can* be challenging to teach. Some children who have this diagnosis will present very little in the way of challenging behaviour. As a teacher, you may experience frustration and might find that some students with this condition take up a disproportionate amount of your time. However, students with this condition can be supported effectively and can achieve in school. You might consider the following strategies:

- Keep 'stress' in the classroom to a minimum
- Use countdowns to ask for quiet
- Be patient and prepared to repeat yourself calmly
- Display classroom rules in clear, precise language
- Allow 'time out' in a safe place
- Make deliberate use of eye contact when speaking
- Allow stress or fiddle toys
- Allow doodling/mind-maps while listening

- Follow classroom routines consistently
- Seat the student near you in the room
- Provide structure – lists, mnemonics, timetables
- Accept that sometimes the behaviour may be uncontrolled
- Talk to them about issues on their own, not in front of the class
- Establish clear systems for classroom talk
- Don't look to correct every instance of unfocused behaviour

ANXIETY AND DEPRESSION

While these terms are medically specific, they have also become 'broad use' terminology for people experiencing a range of difficulties in their sense of well-being. Conditions of this sort vary in their longevity and severity and they are on the increase across the globe (World Health Organisation, 2017). The fact that the terminology is being employed in this manner means that there are still individuals and organisations who do not credit it with the concern, and consequently the support, it merits. There is still stigmatisation, particularly in the workplace, where the struggles a person might experience with such conditions remain wrapped up in their efficacy and value in the working environment.

As teachers, we have to be careful that we don't perpetuate such thinking. Childhood, and particularly adolescence, are emotionally complicated periods in life and children can suffer a range of issues. Students in your classroom may have been exposed to all the very worst that life can offer and may be suffering from trauma-induced emotional issues. Other students may just be experiencing low mood that has very little to do with environmental or situational factors. Others may be in a state of heightened anxiety about relationships, bullying, social status, a mistake or a poor choice. Others may have a developmentally-induced imbalance or may just be medically prone to bouts of depression. This speculative list could continue for some time. Couple this with the achievement-focused stress arising in the classroom and you can begin to see the potentially volatile cocktail that is school combined with modern life.

If you do work to become the kind of teacher in whom students can invest their trust, you may be the recipient of disclosure. It might be that you are the only person in whom that student can confide, or it may just be that you're present when a crisis emerges. If you invest time in your pastoral responsibilities, for example as a form tutor or primary class teacher, the likelihood of this increases. Look to create safe, trusting and supportive relationships with your students – it could well be the case that you end up being the catalyst they need to open up and share what's going on.

As a classroom teacher, look to work sensitively and vigilantly. Don't push a student too hard if they appear to be upset. If somebody appears distracted and that behaviour is not disrupting the room, find a way to chat and gently refocus them. If you notice sudden changes in behaviour, appearance, focus or reactions, aim to understand why, rather than identifying the change as a problem and turning it into an issue of compliance. Take your duty-of-care responsibility seriously and make use of the pastoral support systems and structures available within and outside the school.

REFLECTIVE QUESTION

- Look at the support structures in your placement school. What systems are in place to support your work with children in difficulty?

SENSORY AND/OR PHYSICAL NEEDS

HEARING IMPAIRMENT

The greatest challenge facing a child with a hearing impairment is communication. A child with a hearing impairment is likely to have some hearing as the number of totally deaf children is relatively low. Deafness can be classified as mild, moderate, severe or profound, and the deafness can either be conductive (where sound cannot pass effectively to the auditory nerve, the causes for which may be temporary) or sensori-neural (a fault in the inner ear or auditory nerve and likely to be permanent).

Hearing impairment may lead to difficulties with speech, including being a late starter to talk. Students may also struggle with listening skills, memory, language processing, vocabulary and difficulties with literacy and numeracy. Behaviour, motivation and social interaction can also be affected.

They are likely to be given specialist input and may also have been trained in systems such as Auditory-Aural, Sign-Bilingual or Total Communication (Beattie, 2006; Spencer & Marschark, 2006, 2010).

Although specialist intervention, systems and support are often used, students with hearing impairments can make progress in mainstream classrooms with additional support and adaptation. You might try:

- Seating them at the front with an unobstructed line of vision
- Making use of assistive devices, such as hearing loops
- Reducing background noise in the classroom (seat them away from humming computers)
- Not talking with your back to the window
- Visually indicating who is speaking and allow one speaker at once
- Repeating instructions/questions/student answers
- Facing the student when talking
- Standing still when giving instructions
- Providing all information in written format

- Allowing students to record lessons
- Using subtitles on all audio-visual resources

SIGHT IMPAIRMENT

Sight impairment occurs on a continuum, but does not include children whose sight can be satisfactorily corrected by wearing glasses. This condition can affect comprehension, organisational skills, concentration and task completion, and general academic and social skills. To support these students, you might:

- Choose their seating carefully to maximise their potential sight of resources
- Aim to reduce glare from whiteboards
- Where possible, seat them so that lights are behind or at the side of the student
- Provide enlarged resources
- Use fewer configurations on a page
- Provide lined paper for writing (darker lines are better)
- Provide contrast on visual materials (light/dark)
- Explain any visual materials clearly and simply
- Allow longer to complete tasks
- Avoid ornate fonts

DISADVANTAGED STUDENTS

In many respects, this category of students in this chapter may seem somewhat out of place in this chapter. However, they are included for some very specific reasons. As we have seen earlier, their status as a group requiring additional support and intervention is significant in school accountability systems and is therefore likely to be an area of additional focus and scrutiny in relation to your teaching. Many Initial Teacher Training (ITT) providers will ask you to demonstrate in your planning that these students have been given specific attention.

However, let's clear up a key misconception – there is no such thing as a typical disadvantaged student. The same can be said of many of the obstacles we have encountered in this chapter: each child is unique; generalisations are potentially counterproductive; we should differentiate for potential, not ability, or, in the case of this chapter, preconceived ideas about how a condition is likely to impact on learning.

These considerations are particularly pertinent when it comes to students who are from disadvantaged backgrounds. The word 'disadvantage' implies deprivation, poverty, social and familial disruption and a whole host of other obstacles that might impact on learning. While some of these factors may be influential for some students in receipt of the Pupil Premium Grant (PPG), they may not be for others.

The Ever6 measure might even mean that a student in receipt of the PPG could be living a relatively affluent lifestyle. There may have been a period, a few years earlier, when a separation or divorce required a newly single parent to apply for benefits on a temporary basis. Some students in receipt of the PPG may live in stable, reasonably well-resourced, loving and supportive households where the level of parental earnings means that they are eligible for free school meals.

Additionally, there is no academic profile related to PPG-eligible students. Although, as a group, they do not make the same progress at national levels as their peers, please don't make the mistake of assuming that this means that, as a group, they are less capable. An interesting read on this subject can be found in David Didau's compellingly argued book, *Making Kids Cleverer* (Didau, 2019: chapter 4). Although he takes a very defined stance on the role of knowledge that a number of researchers have contested (you, of course, can make your own mind up), he explains the relationship between IQ, academic performance and the role of environmental factors. The conclusion that he draws is that while certain demographic groups may collectively score lower on IQ tests, this is not genetic (the result of nature), but the product of environmental factors, such as exposure to vocabulary and social factors such as peer groups and cultural experiences (Didau, 2019). To conclude, PPG-eligible students are no less capable than their peers; if we adapt teaching for them, we do it for their potential, not as a perception of ability.

Having said all of this, the PPG exists for a reason: the data shows that students who fall into this category, *as a collective group*, achieve less well than their peers in examination outcomes. Outcomes in your placement schools are likely to reflect this. Students in this group are statistically more likely to present with SEND, to have attendance issues and to be at risk of exclusion. The link between relative poverty, associated social conditions and life chances in our society is well established, and as an individual teacher, you have the opportunity to make a positive impact.

CONCLUSION

You will best support students in tackling their obstacles by combining all the positives of great teaching to create a stable, trusting, structured and aspirational environment in which every student, irrespective of background, feels a sense of belonging and believes that they can achieve. On your plan, this does *not* look like a set of 'one size fits all' interventions targeted at students who are identified as Pupil Premium, or SEND, or poorly behaved, or more able. This is the laziest form of differentiation, is tokenistic in nature and is likely to impact negatively on those whom you target. It is also unnecessary work that is ultimately a waste of your time. As with all of the obstacles that we have considered in this chapter, it is about forming trusting relationships with students, gathering the information you need and supporting them individually to help them succeed.

STRATEGIES FOR SUCCESS

This is the section in which we look at how you might make use of information to support your teaching. Following that, we consider some additional strategies that support the focus of this chapter.

GATHER YOUR INFORMATION

Knowing your students is particularly important in this area of your work. As we have discussed, there will be information available to you as a result of the school meeting its statutory duties, but there will also be the information that you gather through your teaching, through informal conversations and through training.

Start with your class lists and check through the school's information database. Look for students who have been identified as having SpLD and/or an EHCP. Take note of which students have been identified as eligible for the PPG. Compare this information with their prior attainment: to what degree have these potential obstacles impacted on their learning so far? How does this information relate to the expectations outlined by the school (this might be in the form of individual subject target grades in secondary schools, or if they are expected to meet Age-Related Expectations in primary settings)?

Read their school reports from previous terms and/or school years. What conclusions can you draw? Look in their individual profile on the school's information management system. How involved have parents been? What support has been offered? What communications have been sent home that might afford you some more insight? How has the school mapped their provision? Has the student been afforded the opportunity to offer some insight or their views? This might be in the form of a 'learning passport', which is a system used by some schools to outline student preferences and adaptations that have been found to be effective.

If you discover a condition about which you know very little, use all the information you have gathered to consider what support you might offer. Speak to the school's SENDCO and ask for some advice. Access specialist information available in books or online.

Finally, and most importantly, plan to get to know your students as you teach them. Pay attention to their progress and the points at which they seem to experience difficulty. Open up dialogue about this as your working relationship progresses and look to provide them with the personalised support that they need to progress in your classroom.

TIPS FOR SUPPORTING STUDENTS IN OVERCOMING OBSTACLES

- Remember that each student is an individual; they are not defined by their obstacles, their conditions or their social background.

- Look to work responsively and make appropriate adaptations, rather than using generic information about conditions.
- Gather your information proactively.
- Read and learn about how conditions present, then seek to relate what you have learned to the individual, rather than fitting the student to the information.
- Don't plan adaptations for groups of students just because it's quicker and easier to do so, but do so if it works to generate learning.
- Build effective working relationships with students in which they feel comfortable discussing their progress and the difficulties they face.
- Create an inclusive classroom culture in which all differences are respected and supported.

SUMMARY

In this chapter, we have covered:

- The statutory frameworks determining how students with obstacles should be supported.
- Your role as a teacher in meeting these requirements.
- The four areas of need outlined in the *SEN and Disability Code of Practice*.
- Some key obstacles to learning, how they manifest and the support that you might offer in response.
- The importance of respecting the individuality of each student and adapting for their needs, rather than their category.

REFERENCES

Beattie, R. (2006) The oral methods and spoken language. In P. Spencer & M. Marschark (eds), *Advances in the Spoken Language Development of Deaf and Hard-of-Hearing Children*. New York: Oxford University Press.

Bruner, J. (1966) *Toward a Theory of Instruction*. Cambridge, MA: Harvard University Press.

Children and Families Act 2014. Accessed online (6 April 2021) at: www.legislation.gov.uk/ukpga/2014/6/contents/enacted

Department for Education (2011) *Teachers' Standards*. London: HMSO. Accessed online (23 February 2021) at: www.gov.uk/government/publications/teachers-standards

Department for Education (2015) *SEN and Disability Code of Practice 0 to 25 Years*. London: HMSO. Accessed online (6 April 2021) at: www.gov.uk/government/publications/send-code-of-practice-0-to-25

Department for Education (2019) *ITT Core Content Framework*. London: HMSO. Accessed online (23 February 2021) at: www.gov.uk/government/publications/initial-teacher-training-itt-core-content-framework

Department for Education (2021) *Pupil Premium Policy Paper*. London: HMSO. Accessed online (6 April 2021) at: www.gov.uk/government/publications/pupil-premium/pupil-premium

Didau, D. (2019) *Making Kids Cleverer: A Manifesto for Closing the Advantage Gap*. Carmarthen: Crown House Publishing.

Equality Act 2010. Accessed online (6 April 2021) at: www.legislation.gov.uk/ukpga/2010/15/contents

Miles, T. R., & Miles, E. (2004) *Dyslexia and Mathematics* (2nd edn). London: Routledge.

Piaget, J. (1964) Cognitive development in children. *Journal of Research in Science Training*, 2(3), 176–186.

Rose, J. et al. (2009) *Identifying and Teaching Children and Young People with Dyslexia and Literacy Difficulties*. An independent report from Sir Jim Rose to the Secretary of State for Children, Schools and Families. Nottingham: DCSF Publications.

Spencer, P. E., & Marschark, M. (2006) *Advances in the Spoken Language Development of Deaf and Hard-of-Hearing Children*. New York: Oxford University Press.

Spencer, P., & Marschark, M. (2010) Evidence-Based Practice in Educating Deaf and Hard-of-Hearing Students. Oxford University Press.

Vygotsky, L. (1962) *Thought and language*. (E. Hanfmann & G. Vakar, Eds.). MIT Press.

Wing, L., & Gould, J. (1979) Severe impairments of social interaction and associated abnormalities in children: Epidemiology and classification. *Journal of Autism and Developmental Disorders*, 9, 11–29.

World Health Organisation (2017) *Mental Health*. Geneva: WHO. Accessed online (23 February 2021) at: www.who.int/health-topics/mental-health#tab=tab_1

6

ADAPTIVE TEACHING

IN THIS CHAPTER, WE WILL COVER:

- Why do we adapt our teaching to meet individual needs?
- How do we adapt for potential, not ability, and why is this important?
- What is the difference between reactive and proactive differentiation?
- What are adaptive teaching strategies and how might they be deployed?

INTRODUCTION

Of all the chapters in this book, this is the one that illustrates the three guiding principles with the most clarity. As we begin our careers, we seek to plan lessons that will engage, excite, entertain and energise the students. We teach the plan, we teach the room, we teach the lesson, *but do we teach the students*? What have they learnt?

Differentiation, at its root, is the practice of meeting the needs of every individual in the room. This is the true art of teaching and it is not without challenge. Modern classrooms may have 35 students (or more). In a 50-minute lesson this would be at best one minute's attention per individual. How can a teacher even begin to approach the complexity of this task with the resources available?

In this chapter, we look at the reasons why teachers need to adapt their lessons to meet the needs of individual students. Following that, we explore the concept of adapting for potential, not for ability. We then investigate two different approaches to adaptation, identifying the difference between working proactively and reactively. We then conclude by considering some key strategies that you might employ.

It's important to make clear at the outset that attempting to deliver a personally designed lesson for every student, every lesson, is not achievable. Trainees often feel this pressure. We can, however, plan and teach in a way that is responsive to the needs that we know about in advance. We can also deliver the learning in a way that is flexible to needs as they arise. The requirement for thinking in this manner is embedded in both the *Teachers' Standards* (TS5) (Department for Education, 2011) and, subsequently, in the *ITT Core Content Framework* (Department for Education, 2019).

ITT CORE CONTENT FRAMEWORK

The *Core Content Framework* (CCF) (Department for Education, 2019: 20–21) makes some very clear statements about differentiation, under the 'Learn that' headings for Teachers' Standard 5 (Department for Education, 2011):

1. Students are likely to learn at different rates and to require different levels and types of support from teachers to succeed.
2. Seeking to understand students' differences, including their different levels of prior knowledge and potential barriers to learning, is an essential part of teaching.
3. Adapting teaching in a responsive way, including by providing targeted support to students who are struggling, is likely to increase student success.
4. Adaptive teaching is less likely to be valuable if it causes the teacher to artificially create distinct tasks for different groups of students or to set lower expectations for particular students.

5. Flexibly grouping students within a class to provide more tailored support can be effective, but care should be taken to monitor its impact on engagement and motivation, particularly for low attaining students.
6. There is a common misconception that students have distinct and identifiable learning styles. This is not supported by evidence and attempting to tailor lessons to learning styles is unlikely to be beneficial.
7. Students with special educational needs or disabilities are likely to require additional or adapted support; working closely with colleagues, families and students to understand barriers and identify effective strategies is essential.

Let's give some thought to these statements – they are rich with information and no small amount of technicality. Statement 1 asks us to consider the pace at which students learn and how this might impact on our teaching. It's important to note here that the pace at which students learn is not fixed. The evidence suggests that students go through both surges and dips in their progress. Keeping abreast of this in a full class requires some vigilance.

A very important point to note at this stage is that adaptation is not just a deficit model. As well as providing additional support for those students who need it, we should also be thinking about how we build in stretch and challenge for those who are progressing really quickly.

Statement 2 focuses on understanding difference and has a very close relationship with our guiding principles, as well as with the 'Gather your information' sections at the close of our chapters. As we work our way through this chapter you will begin to recognise that this amounts to more than just lofty idealism; if you want to develop your teaching to a high standard, you simply must begin to think in this manner.

REFLECTIVE QUESTION

- What routines might a teacher employ that ensure that they build compensation for difference into their planning?

Statements 3, 4 and 5 urge some caution in relation to this process. These statements arise from both research and from a political desire to ensure that low-attaining students receive the same aspirational teaching as their peers. It's explicit within these statements that setting 'different' work is not desirable, so how then does a teacher 'differentiate'?

Statement 6 can be misinterpreted and is worth some clarification. 'Learning styles' as a guiding approach for teaching has seen several incarnations. If you want to understand more, you can look at Honey and Mumford (1982). A common confusion in this area is found in relating these ideas to those of Howard Gardner (2011). It is worth noting that Gardner's 'Multiple Intelligence Theory' has been widely misinterpreted when applied as a 'learning style'-based methodology. The 'styles' offered were Visual, Auditory and Kinesthetic or, in Gardener's case, amounted to nine separate but connected 'intelligences', ranging from Interpersonal to Linguistic and Musical. Gardner's work has numerous applications in the classroom and the research related to this thinking continues.

The statement in the CCF does not arise from any inherent lack of validity to these ideas. It is true to say that as human beings, we all learn differently and have our preferred ways of approaching new tasks and information. What the statement does imply is that the application of these ideas as rigid constructs in the classroom is not supported by the evidence as being beneficial to learning (Nancekivell, Shah & Gelman, 2019). Put another way, designing visual lessons for visual students, or social lessons for interpersonal students is not going to support meaningful learning. This is correct. You cannot create activities for a student who has linguistic strengths and a separate lesson for one who has a more visual inclination, without denying each student another means of accessing the information. The evidence suggests that limiting students in this manner limits the learning. Consequently, it's important to recognise that we all learn differently. As teachers, we might make adaptions for that, but that we should aim for the full range of stimuli for all students if we want to deepen the learning for all. Think 'multi-sensory' and you will be heading in the right direction.

REFLECTIVE QUESTION

- Think of an area of subject content that you will teach on your training programme. How many different ways might you present the material, ensuring a multi-sensory approach?

Statement 7 is given greater consideration in Chapter 5 on obstacles to learning, but this is likely to be one of your primary considerations when planning differentiation for your classes. It requires specialist and student-based knowledge, all of which can be gained if you follow the strategies for success outlined in both this chapter and others.

We might think of it in this way: at any given point in the lesson, there will be students who require no differentiation; there will be some who require some additional support; there will be some who require greater challenge. This shifts frequently, according to task, time, student and context. Staying alert and practising vigilance are key, as well as accumulating knowledge about the individuals in the room – know your students. If we don't do it enough, we run the risk of treating every student as if they are the same; if we try to do too much, the result is likely to be chaotic.

We will finish this section by making a quick observation about terminology. The language used in official documentation has veered away from use of the term 'differentiation' and instead uses 'adaptation'. It is my intention to use them interchangeably during this chapter. The national thinking on differentiation has moved on recently and is now being reframed. There is a view in some circles that differentiation is both unrealistic and unhelpful, but that view does not extend to adapting your teaching to meet individual needs. I take the view that this language distinction is not necessary, and that we might organise our thinking slightly differently. This is addressed in the section on proactive and reactive differentiation.

ABILITY, POTENTIAL AND GROWTH

Earlier, we mentioned that the research demonstrates that students can learn at different paces according to context. Contextual factors affecting learning might include: emotional state, view of the lesson content, experiences in previous lessons, time of day, physical condition, situation at home, what just happened in the playground, what happened in the last lesson, nutrition intake that day, hydration, seating, room temperature, hormonal state, view of own efficacy, level of motivation – the list is potentially endless and will vary from student to student. Some of those might be short-term issues that affect performance on a given day at a specific time, but others may be more pervasive and impactful over longer periods.

The pace of learning demonstrated by a student on our first few encounters may well lead us to conclude a number of things about that student. This might have been further reinforced by a conversation with a colleague in the staffroom. We might form a fixed view of that student's ability and begin to modify our teaching to that view. In effect, we conflate current performance with our perception of the student's ability or intelligence. The student is likely to pick up on this and it will inform their perception of what you think of them. They then start to work to that expectation. This cycle then repeats and comes to represent a 'glass ceiling' for their development. In essence, your influential position as a teacher shapes that student's view of themselves and their efficacy in your classroom.

It is worth us taking a pause here to consider what we understand by the term 'ability'. Culturally, we invest in the idea of ability in a number of ways. We think of ability, or intelligence, as being a pre-determined quality that some people are born with and others are not. The language in schools reflects this; we refer to 'more able' students. This thinking has a background in 'intelligence testing'.

One of the ways in which we test intelligence and ascribe a value to it is through IQ tests. IQ finds its origins in tests, developed by Binet and Simon (1905), that were initially developed as a measuring system to identify children who were failing to progress in the school system, so that they might be given additional support. The tests included word definitions, comprehension activities, reasoning assessment and numerical capacity. IQ testing was a system that arose from this original set of tests: chronological age was measured against 'mental age', producing a ratio described as 'Intelligence Quotient'. Labelling people in this manner continues to be controversial to this day. Binet died before IQ was introduced as a concept, but Simon described this as a betrayal of their initial intentions (Gregory, 1992). During the First World War, Cyril Burt, a psychologist, further developed this idea as a means of attributing people to work roles suitable to their abilities. His view was that intelligence was fixed, unchanging and measurable.

Numerous methods of measuring 'intelligence' as a fixed entity have been developed subsequently, with different areas of focus and varied methodologies. None of them is universally accepted to be accurate, due to issues of either reliability (producing the same results repeatedly) or validity (producing the same results as other tests). There are tests with an over-emphasis on verbal ability, tests that fail to take account of social context, and tests that fail to compensate for a Specific Learning Difficulty (SpLD), such as dyslexia. For further reading on this topic, look at the work of Gardner (2011), Spearman (1927) and Sternberg (1999).

The concept of intelligence continues to underpin educational policy, particularly as it relates to assessment and curriculum design, both of which are pertinent to the trainee teacher's classroom. What if we start to think of ability, or to use another term, intelligence, as an unfixed quality? What if we start to think of intelligence, or ability, as expandable? It doesn't take long, when thinking about this, to realise the profound implications of such a question for the way in which we organise schooling and the manner in which a teacher might operate in the classroom.

REFLECTIVE QUESTION

• Do you believe that people can increase their intelligence? What basis do you have for your belief?

Lucas and Claxton, Professors at the University of Winchester and founder members of the Expansive Education Network, have focused their research on exploring some of these issues. In two compelling books, *New Kinds of Smart* (Lucas & Claxton, 2010) and *Expansive Education* (Lucas, Claxton & Spencer, 2013), they make the case for reviewing our understanding of ability, or intelligence, and subsequently, changing our pedagogical approaches. Drawing on Educational Psychology and research into the science of learning, they explain that we should rethink our notion of intelligence as fixed and begin to think of it as expandable. By expandable, they mean that students can 'learn how to learn' more effectively through developing metacognitive skills (see Chapter 3 on learning) and developing 'habits of mind' that they find improve their capacity for engagement with new concepts and skills.

They argue that the teacher has a key role in facilitating this process. First, a teacher needs to support the cultivation of key learning dispositions, one of which is a 'growth mindsets'. Based on the work of Carol Dweck (2006), this proposes the notion that if people believe themselves to be able to increase their intelligence, they are very likely to do so. By shifting our own language and by helping students to recognise and articulate where and how they experience success, we can support them to become more effective learners and subsequently experience greater measurable success.

Second, we need to manage our classroom in a way that communicates to our students that we believe they all have the potential to expand their abilities at all times. How might we do this?

There are implications for the language we use. How do we describe ability? Do we refer to the more able? Do you refer to some students as clever? How do we frame a student's struggle to master a skill or concept? Is it because it is 'beyond them'? Employing a growth mindset means that we use the language of possibility and aspiration, rather than the language of limitation.

REFLECTIVE QUESTION

- If we aspire to stop using words like 'ability', with what might we replace it?

We need to think carefully about the tasks that we set, the manner in which they are explained, how they are modelled, the support we provide in their completion and who gets that support, as well as at what point in proceedings. If we have built in appropriate challenge (see Vygotsky's (1934) Zone of Proximal Development), then our students should be feeling stretched, but not overwhelmed. Sometimes they succeed alone, sometimes they succeed with our help, and sometimes they don't succeed. Getting things wrong has to be a key part of the learning – this is what Doug Lemov (2010) refers to as a 'culture of error'.

We communicate what we value in the classroom – rewards and praise support us with this. However, what do we reward? Do we praise the student who is quickest to answer, who always knows the answer and experiences the greatest and most rapid success? Or should we be rewarding the dispositions that we hope to cultivate among our learners? Do we reward resilience, tenacity, bravery, willingness? As well as praise, how do we employ feedback to communicate the value of these dispositions? Is it that a student 'hasn't understood', or that they 'haven't understood it *yet*'?

Needless to say, there is nothing to be gained from forming a fixed view of a child's ability and then working to that. If we talk less and listen more, we might move towards a revised view of students' abilities and begin to really understand how we might differentiate in a way that promotes aspiration, as illustrated in the case study below.

CASE STUDY: ADAPTING FOR POTENTIAL, NOT ABILITY

Poppy, a primary student in Yorkshire, was really struggling with the primary curriculum. Her reading seemed to be very slow and included short periods of time, up to 20 seconds, when she just seemed to go blank. She seemed unable to recall any words by sight, even ones that were repeated within the same sentence. At the age of 6, she still could not recognise numbers up to 10. The impact on Poppy's learning experience was profound.

Teachers at the school formed the view that the issue was one of ability and described Poppy as a child who finds it 'difficult to learn'. Lots of well-intentioned interventions were put in place. When, in Year 2, Poppy was given material for Year 1 students, she was withdrawn from some lessons for additional reading support, which mainly consisted of additional time spent reading to an adult. She undertook much of her learning with Year 1 students and began to form the view that she was unable to learn in the same way and at the same speed as her peers. She developed a sense of the difference between herself and other children and ultimately began to form a negative view of school.

Fortunately for Poppy, she had parents who supported her education and advocated on her behalf. Poppy's mum was dyslexic and she recognised much of what Poppy was experiencing. Poppy was assessed and found to have dyslexia. This is no surprise: phonic decoding (converting symbols into sounds/abstract ideas) is problematic for dyslexic students. The bulk of the primary curriculum is, of course, delivered through text. Reading for dyslexic children can be slower, is likely to be characterised by misreading at points, and consequently, tasks are completed more slowly, with answers having a greater degree of inaccuracy.

It is not difficult to see how a teacher characterised Poppy as somebody who struggles with learning, works at a slower pace and might tend towards unfocused and/or disruptive behaviours, and then began to differentiate on that basis. However, once Poppy was assessed, it was also clear that Poppy had above-average cognitive ability and some key strengths in her vocabulary range, her visual ability, as well as her interpersonal skills.

The teacher's view of Poppy was radically altered by the outcome of the test. Rather than perceiving Poppy as a child who was unlikely to progress, she began to differentiate to foster the potential that some of the test outcomes indicated. Poppy was given different processes to support her difficulties with phonic processing, including 'overlearning', resources that maximised her visual skills and different reading strategies. Rather than simply making everything easier for Poppy, including giving her work suitable for younger students, the teacher began to challenge Poppy to realise her potential, to speak the language of success and to build her motivation in tackling the issues presented by her dyslexia. In essence, rather than differentiating in a manner that communicated to Poppy that she couldn't do what other children could do, she began to communicate that Poppy could do it, with the right support and effort.

The impact: Poppy began to make much more rapid progress than she had previously. She began to develop self-belief and determination to succeed. She grew in confidence and began to request work with more challenge, and, most importantly, she began to talk about enjoying school.

The important thing to note here is that it was not the assessment that changed Poppy's progress and enjoyment for the better, it was the teacher's shift in perception: she moved from a deficit model in which she sought to provide work commensurate with her assessment of Poppy's ability, to a model in which she sought to unlock Poppy's potential. While the assessment made it clear that Poppy had this potential, had the teacher worked on this basis from the outset, focusing on Poppy's presenting capabilities and how best to maximise them, Poppy may have begun to progress more quickly irrespective of any assessment taking place. The focus moves away from a perception of *ability* (as it currently presents) and towards working to *potential*.

REACTIVE AND PROACTIVE DIFFERENTIATION - THE DIFFERENCE

As we saw earlier in the chapter, the *Core Content Framework* includes the following statement:

> Adaptive teaching is less likely to be valuable if it causes the teacher to artificially create distinct tasks for different groups of students or to set lower expectations for particular students. (Department for Education, 2019: 20)

The implications of this are significant when considered against the background of differentiated practice in classrooms during the last 20 years or so. Differentiation of a particular kind seems to be something that the Department for Education no longer welcomes. A question arises: can we differentiate if we don't create distinctive tasks? Implicit within the statement is the notion that to do so somehow lowers expectations. Let's pick this apart and consider the implications for our adaptive practice.

First, the answer to the question is yes, you can. There are a variety of different ways in which you can differentiate that don't always involve setting different tasks.

Some of these are covered in detail in the section of this chapter entitled 'Adaptive teaching strategies'.

The second point refers to the lowering of expectations. Does setting a different task lower expectation?

If you are working with a classroom full of students with differing rates of progress, you will be required to adapt your teaching to meet their needs. One way in which we can do this is to set a different task. An example might be a primary maths lesson in which the students are learning about coordinates. The teacher has explained how to use the x and y axis to calculate the coordinates of a specified location on the grid. Questions, of increasing difficulty, challenge the students to use their new knowledge and plot coordinates accurately. To increase difficulty, negative axes are introduced, and after some more modelling from the teacher, the students begin the work.

Four of the students become unable to progress at this point. The introduction of the negative axes has challenged their abstract reasoning skills and they simply don't understand how to use them in conjunction with the positive axes. What are your options at this point? If you are differentiating for ability, you may have anticipated this prior to the lesson and produced separate worksheets that don't contain the negative axis work. Another way of looking at this (or perhaps justifying it) would be to set the negative axis as extension work for those who complete the positive axis questions. However, the negative axis is on the curriculum, so doesn't this amount to withholding some vital material? The counterview is that trying to introduce more challenging concepts, when it might be wiser to consolidate, could result in cognitive overload.

Quite the dilemma. And it's easy to see how the CCF arrives at a strong statement of this kind. There is another approach, and rather than working proactively as described above (anticipating limitations prior to the lesson and creating a separate learning plan), you might work responsively. What would this look like? It would be to use your knowledge of the students to anticipate the difficulties that might arise, and to target the students for additional support in a number of ways.

You might provide them with some additional instruction/clarification as you circulate the room following the initial explanations and modelling. You might ensure that your route around the room prioritises these students. You might seat them together so that you can offer some additional modelling and/or instruction while the rest of the class continues to work. You might, during your questioning following your initial instructions, ask them some questions that engage their explanatory thinking, giving them an additional opportunity to process the ideas through explanation. You might, once you are working with the small group, scaffold the material by completing part of the process for them and then ask them to complete it. Following this, they then complete one independently.

After all of this, they may still be struggling to fully grasp some of the concepts, but they have had the opportunity, they have been exposed to the content, they have employed their existing knowledge and they have some pride in having attempted the challenging work, building their sense of self-efficacy and strengthening their overall learning dispositions. One key message that they have not received: 'You can't do what other people can.'

I want to be clear at this point: this doesn't mean that we don't differentiate. The term 'adaptive teaching' has different connotations in educational literature from those associated with differentiation. Key thinkers such as E. D. Hirsch (2016) and David Didau (2019) have made some very strong statements about differentiation in recent years (although their rationales are very different). There is a great deal of validity to two of their key arguments: differentiation is an unrealistic burden on the teacher, and differentiated resources impose limitations on students that amount to a restriction of learning. However, it would be a leap to state that we should *never* differentiate by providing different resources. There may well be circumstances in which, used sparingly, compassionately and smartly, it may support a struggling student to make progress.

An example might be a student who works really well independently, but doesn't respond particularly well when offered one-to-one support. You might produce a resource that is pre-scaffolded to support their progress to the final endpoint. You haven't given them a different task; you've just given them additional support on the way there. Another example might be a student who struggles to concentrate during verbal instruction and modelling. You might provide a resource that consolidates the instructions, with some extra visual prompts that other students may not require. It's worth noting that while you have provided extra/different resources in these examples, you have not lowered your expectations and have continued to teach in a way that encourages the potential success of the student.

ADAPTIVE TEACHING STRATEGIES

In this section, we will look at a range of adaptive strategies. Some of them will be responsive in nature, but there are some proactive strategies that you might also employ. In all of the examples provided, please keep in mind the need to differentiate for potential, not for ability. The categories of differentiation shared in this chapter are by no means exhaustive, nor are they mutually exclusive, but they should give you food for thought and enable you to begin the process of adapting your teaching to meet the needs of your students. Let's consider some of the ways in which you might begin to approach this challenge.

ADAPTATION BY GROUPING

Group work has its advocates and those who just won't use it. In some subjects, it's a critical skill, such as PE, drama and citizenship. In drama, as much as 60% of a GCSE grade could hinge on a term-long devising project. Learning collaboratively has many benefits, with ideas rooted in the thinking of psychologists such as Vygotsky (1934) and Dewey (1916/2011), who both considered learning to be a social enterprise. This material is covered in Chapter 3 on learning. In this chapter, we focus exclusively on its role as an adaptive tool.

Put any group of human beings together in a pressurised, achievement-based activity and it won't be long before the tensions start to rise. It's important that proactive adaptation processes mitigate for this by meeting individual student needs through careful group configuration.

A drama teacher in Leicester (Miss Khan) developed quite a sophisticated system to ensure that grouping was maximally beneficial to groups of teenagers. Over the years, through careful observation and reflection, she began to group the students more effectively. She also learnt to manage the creative process and the continued cohesion of groups to greater effect. The methods she used are essentially proactive adaptation in action, and therefore relevant to a variety of situations in which group work might feature.

The groups were carefully designed. She organised the students on a spreadsheet, creating columns for focus, creativity, leadership, attendance, understanding, maturity, aptitudes and artistic style. These columns changed annually as she explored new ways of working. Each category was scored out of 10: rudimentary, yes, but this was quite a useful method for categorising. She then used the scoring to sort the groups so that there was numerical consistency in each category across the groups.

Finally, and more importantly, she then looked at the individuals – did each group make sense in terms of social interaction, personality types, etc? It didn't always work. In fact, on a number of occasions it crashed and burned spectacularly. But on the whole, she did manage to avoid the classic drama teacher pitfall of group meltdown and the impact on results was tangible, compared to classes in the same school that didn't employ these processes.

Once the students are grouped (and by group we mean anything from two students upwards), the adaptive opportunities are numerous. Imagine placing two students together who have an advanced understanding of the material – what could they gain from working together? Is there a great opportunity for stretch and challenge here? Conversely, what advantage might be gleaned from placing a group of students together who need to consolidate their understanding of some key concepts?

Imagine grouped responses to questions – a wonderful way of building confidence in the classroom. You ask a question, give some thinking time, allow the group to discuss and then one of them offers the group's response to the rest of the class. We can call this 'think–group–share'. Students benefit from testing out their thinking in a relatively safe context, fostering greater engagement and boosting confidence.

Imagine a carefully selected group of students working together on a project in which their different aptitudes and qualities combine to create an outcome that they deliver with pride – it's hard to conceive of better preparation for the world of work.

Groups could potentially be organised by considering: interests, social interests, learning needs, leadership skills, social groups, working pace, concentration and focus, personalities, resilience, confidence, tenacity and so on.

In such a group, would they all play the same role? The dynamics of human interaction suggest that this would be very unlikely, which leads us to our next form of adaptation: by responsibility.

ADAPTATION BY RESPONSIBILITY

Each student has different strengths and areas for development. As we have discussed, any work that involves interaction between students can be used to enhance learning, if the groupings or pairings are carefully matched to this understanding of your students. This is the real benefit of mixed-ability classes.

One of the immediate consequences is that it puts students in the position of the teacher. Inevitably, understanding of the task and the content will be varied within the group and some students will need to take on the responsibility of explaining this to others, or, to put it bluntly, do some teaching – an excellent opportunity to challenge. To teach means to break down information and make it accessible. To do so, you have to really organise your own thinking. You will be asked questions that mean you have to reorganise that information once again to help somebody else understand. This may be done by re-articulating, restructuring, drawing comparisons, creating analogies – the strategies are endless. There is a great deal of skill in this process and empowering students to think and behave in this way really develops their understanding of the material. They will develop additional structure around their own understanding through applying what they know, moving further along the scale from novice to expert.

This takes care of those who are ahead of the game by providing one form of extra challenge. Furthermore, you could provide them additional stretch and challenge activities. Rather than providing more of the same in terms of consolidation, they could be engaged in stretching the material for the group by exploring more advanced concepts or higher-level knowledge. Other challenges you might include are taking on a leadership role or being responsible for organising and structuring the group's final product.

Students can be given a range of different responsibilities within groups that play to their strengths or areas that you want to develop. Students might undertake research into comparative information. They might record the group's progress and development so that it can be shared with the class. They may organise the group's work schedule, working strategically to ensure that the work is completed to a good standard. They might prepare a presentation that summarises the key ideas. They might be a very effective scribe or minute-taker. They could have artistic or dramatic skills that help communicate the ideas of the group. The range of possibilities is long, but if you aim to play to their strengths, while also looking to adapt in a way that develops their knowledge and skills, adaptation by responsibility can yield some really positive outcomes.

ADAPTATION BY TASK

This is one form of adaptation that has generated some variable practice in the past. As we have seen, proactive differentiation that involves a teacher in preparing multiple resources for students is not recommended in the CCF as it creates a lot of extra work and the end result might be that you suppress progress, despite your good intentions and diligence. Nevertheless, many schools still adopt proactive differentiation as a centralised approach. A very high-performing multi-academy trust in the UK requires teachers to prepare three routes through the learning of every lesson and to allocate one of the three to each student according to progress. It is positively framed, but could be seen as a blunt instrument that creates an ability hierarchy in the classroom.

Having said that, we have seen in adaptation by responsibility that you can vary the tasks or foci for students in a way that both challenges and supports. There are times when it might also be useful to set individual tasks for students, based on who they are, the skills they possess and their response to the learning. Consider the case study below.

CASE STUDY: FINDING WAYS TO ENABLE STUDENTS TO USE THEIR STRENGTHS

Mr Driver taught RS to a Year 11 group in North London. They were studying Buddhism and he had approached the topic at a conversational level, exploring the ideas. The majority of the class were engaged, but there was a group of boys who were finding the whole process very dull; one in particular, Adil, was quite vocal about it. He inevitably began to misbehave, resulting in a 'laying down the law' conversation outside the classroom door. He reacted quite badly, stating the subject was 'long' (arduous and boring) and opted to walk off. Mr Driver watched him walk away and experienced a sense of failure, inevitably.

A few days later the school held an impromptu lunchtime charity talent show and Mr Driver happened to be on duty in the hall. Adil turned up with a couple of mates and to Mr Driver's absolute amazement, performed an incredible rap about the value of the charity for which money was being raised.

He sought Adil out the next day and, you guessed it, asked him to do a rap about Buddhism. You will hear about 'trendy' teachers getting the 'kids' to 'do a rap' about the topic, no doubt inspired by a desire to reach the students 'at their level'. There is some criticism for working in this way among those with a more traditional outlook, but there is no real harm in this approach, as long as there is stretch built in. Let's think about what's

---

involved in writing a rap: linguistic dexterity, rhyming structures, timing, syntax, confidence, rhythm. This skill has real merit when it comes to organising information and the additional benefit of being memorable for those to whom it is performed.

It wouldn't have been enough for Mr Driver to say 'just do a rap'. First, Adil took some persuading and had to be incentivised. The activity was social in nature. Adil had worked with another student and they had bounced off each other during the rap. Mr Driver asked him if anybody in the class could do this. He said not, but that he could have a go at teaching another student how to do it. Adil chose a focused and motivated student whom he admired for his ability to explain ideas. When spoken to about taking part, the student was visibly flattered and very excited about the prospect.

Mr Driver built in a responsibility. They hadn't yet covered 'desire and suffering'. The task was to produce a rap that explained the relationship between these concepts. Adil needed to produce visual aids, including a Karaoke-style presentation, so that everybody could understand the rap, take it away and digest it. Adil and his partner were given some time in the school recording studio with a sixth form mentor, which the Head of Music kindly agreed to supervise. Beats were written, lyrics were written, performance and visual aids were prepared. They came back with a powerful piece of spoken music about the nature of materialism, which was then related to the concept of suffering through constant desire, grounded in some very thorough reading and some careful supervision by Mr Driver. The class loved it. They understood the key concepts, Mr Driver recorded it and played it to other classes as a teaching resource. Adil never walked out in frustration again.

The key to differentiating by task is to understand that everybody receives and processes new information in different ways. If we think carefully about our students and look for new and interesting ways to engage them, we can adapt tasks in a way that supports learning rather than limiting it or creating ability hierarchies that suppress engagement. This is not a 'learning styles' argument; this is about variety, engagement and appropriate challenge in the learning.

It is good practice to 'mix it up' and keep things lively with a wide range of activities, and many teachers do this to excellent effect. However, don't let the resulting engagement fool you into thinking that you have automatically secured great progress as a result.

I once watched a highly engaging lesson during an Ofsted inspection. I had accompanied the lead inspector as an SLT (Senior Leadership Team) member and we were in the process of verifying each other's judgements (the inspector was of the view that this was a one-way process). I watched the lesson unfold. The activities were imaginative, varied and pacey. The students were fully absorbed in the tasks. I was impressed and formed the view that while it wasn't outstanding, it was a very strong good.

Later, the inspector and I picked apart what we had seen. I told him what my judgement was and his response was 'I think you are being over generous. I think it's a 3 approaching a 2'. I was astonished. As he explained his thinking, I realised he was right. He had the evidence carefully summarised. He had seen a highly competent and skilled teacher in action, who would no doubt produce consistently good results with the students. He had seen an imaginative approach to engaging the students in the material. What he had not seen was students assimilating information and building understanding at a sufficient rate, because the lesson structure had not explicitly planned for this to occur. It had simply planned to share the information in a variety of interesting ways. This was an important moment of understanding for me – razzmatazz and fun, although desirable, do not automatically equal learning.

Plan the activities carefully so that learning is at the core. For example, students might be engaged in a science experiment. The experiment may be to discover what happens when you combine magnesium with another chemical. This experiment might be done in groups of three. You might differentiate the tasks according to the strengths of the students. All three might plan the experiment. One then draws a diagram of the process as they progress, another might conduct the experiment itself and the third might record the results. An astute teacher will select the right person for the right task, ensuring that this maximises engagement for all and builds in stretch and challenge suited to the current level of progress and understanding. All three students in this scenario would then be required to produce a final evaluation of the results. You will notice that this has some crossover with adaptation by responsibility. The categories in this chapter are created to aid your understanding; they are not mutually exclusive and should be used as a suite of complementary tools.

ADAPTATION BY PACE

Know your students. The pace that different people work at varies hugely, and the pace at which different people approach different tasks does also. Our enthusiasm for any given scenario affects our approach to it, as does our sense of our own efficacy in that scenario. Our enthusiasm and sense of efficacy may be the result of previous experiences or simply our preferences. Couple these with the variety in learning pace experienced by young people as a result of their development and their social conditions and you will begin to appreciate that learning can never be regarded as an unbroken line of trajectory: it stutters, it fluctuates, it can stop and then it can accelerate again. From this realisation arises the need for an adaptive approach in relation to pace.

This manifests in numerous ways. An observant teacher will come to learn which students rush their way through the work and consequently litter their efforts with mistakes. It may be born out of a desire to get it done as quickly as possible. Such a student might be supported by an instruction to make full use of the time and be given some proofreading strategies. In essence, they are being asked to slow down.

Some students may take longer to digest information. You can create more time for these students in various ways. They might be sent reading materials prior to the lesson to allow them additional familiarisation time. Instructions given out in the class might be supported by a visual guide or a flowchart, or repeated one-to-one, possibly by a teaching assistant.

Some students may need longer to complete written work. You might produce scaffolds that support them with sentence starters or a suggested structure. You might alter the format in which they are required to present their work. It might be that a scribe may be beneficial and a teaching assistant could be assigned this role for periods of the lesson. Try to configure the tasks in a way that ensures the learning is not limited by the adaptations you offer the student. It can be challenging, and you won't always be successful, but aim to provide the same aspiration for them.

It is sometimes necessary to alter the pace of learning for particular groups, if you know that they will need longer to engage fully with the learning. The group could work together, with some additional support, and be given additional time to complete the tasks. To do so, you will need to carefully consider the impact on the learning. What happens to the rest of the group while they continue working? The obvious answer here is that the rest of the group deepens their learning. It could be through an extension task that involves greater depth or increased sophistication. In a primary maths lesson, for example, the slower group might answer fewer questions, but be offered more directed support, while the quicker groups are given greater opportunity to practise their new skills with independent, challenging questions.

It is wise to accommodate these varying needs if you want to ensure that the learning is maximised for all. Learn to be flexible in the way that you organise a lesson. Create time and maximise time.

ADAPTATION BY QUESTIONING AND DISCUSSION

Let's begin by asking ourselves why we ask questions. Most teachers, when asked about this, will describe questioning as having a role in checking on the learning, and they are absolutely correct. It is one of the best means we have at our disposal when ascertaining how much has been understood.

Questions can be used for much more than this, though. Imagine the student who is not a confident speaker (this might be many of our students in reality, and it might include you) and imagine their experience in relation to the 'learning checking' approach to questioning. They may opt to be a passive observer in a room where the right answer is always celebrated, and the same few students provide those answers to the teacher's satisfaction. You can almost hear them thinking, 'Why bother?'

Consider, then, a classroom culture in which the questions don't just check the learning, they also generate it. Consider a classroom in which instruction is lean and economical, but purposeful, and *the teacher talks less and listens more*. In this classroom, there is genuine dialogue about the learning material. The teacher has genuine interest in what the students have to say: their opinions, thoughts and questions open up avenues of discussion that prise open the learning from multiple perspectives. There is speculation, rumination, exploration, analysis, application, synthesis and debate.

In this classroom, where the 'pressure to be right' is reduced, a student might feel more inclined to contribute. A skilful teacher in such a setting might also pitch their questions in a way that supports that student's current level of understanding, enabling them to build confidence and constructing discussion in a manner that genuinely consolidates the learning. If you start to work in this manner, you are already adapting your teaching to meet the needs of your less confident students. Robin Alexander provides some excellent guidance to this approach in his book *A Dialogic Teaching Companion* (Alexander, 2020). One powerful change that can be introduced and will facilitate this process is use of the word 'might'. Here is the same question, phrased differently:

- Can somebody tell me what Conservatism is?
- What *might* Conservatism mean?

The second of the two options allows for a wider range of responses. It invites speculation. It supports incorrect attempts. It opens the notion that there might be more than one possible response, and some room for debate. It invites an entirely different conversation.

In addition, the three-tier-thinking model presented in Chapter 4 on objective-led planning can support you in pitching your questions at a level suited to your students' progress in understanding the material. Students who are still assimilating the knowledge can be asked explanatory questions to scaffold their understanding, students who have a secure grasp of the key concepts may be invited to apply their learning through questions, while one who has progressed very quickly and sees the whole picture might receive a critical thinking question.

You might also seek to use the three-tier-thinking model in a fluid manner to adapt for individuals and groups. A critical thinking question might be posed to the whole group in order to introduce additional challenge, and then groups might work together to respond to an applied question related to the original critical question. They formulate their response together, making use of their combined knowledge and understanding to build a coherent picture. The class then comes back together with their applied responses, at which point the critical thinking question is posed once more and they respond together.

Working in this manner allows you to adapt your teaching flexibly, weaving together different adaptation strategies to meet the needs of both individuals and groups of students.

ADAPTATION BY SCAFFOLDING

This particular strategy is about knowing when to step in to help a student and to what level that help should extend. Scaffolding essentially means providing additional structure and/or information that forms part of the overall picture for the student. It requires us to think of the content in separate 'chunks' and to recognise that sometimes breaking material down into these chunks can facilitate understanding of the whole.

Scaffolding can be offered to individuals or groups, and can be either proactive or reactive in nature. In the reactive example below, scaffolding is envisaged as support given to students once a task has been set and the class is working independently, either individually or in groups. The teacher circulates, checking on progress. Support at this stage might be targeted (proactively, using information previously acquired, the teacher knows who to support first) or it might be in response to what the teacher sees (reactively, as a result of work-checking or other visual indicators such as distraction or a head on a desk). It might take the form of additional instruction, explanation, question or resource.

For example, imagine a Year 6 maths lesson in which the students are working on worded number problems. Such a problem might look like this:

> Simra posts three large letters. The postage costs the same for each letter. She pays with a £20 note. Her change is £12.89. What is the cost of posting one letter?

A question such as this requires a student to employ several skills. First, literacy has to be used to understand the meaning of the question. Second, imagination is employed to visualise the scenario created by the question. It will be easier to answer if the student can picture Simra in the shop, posting her letters: the information can be organised visually as a scenario, moving from abstract concept to relatable experience.

The number problem itself has stages. First, the student must recognise that the change received indicates the amount spent, and that the amount spent relates to the £20 given. They then need to use their numeracy skills to decide which operation must be employed to calculate that amount – in this case, a subtraction. This results in a need to perform the subtraction accurately to arrive at £7.11. Subsequently, they need to recognise that the £7.11 needs to be divided by 3, which in turn requires them to understand that this amount is the amount spent on 3 letters, necessitating that their literacy and imagination are brought to bear once more.

An informed teacher who gathers their information about their classes carefully will be able to identify where individuals might struggle with this process. They might scaffold by describing the shop to facilitate the scenario, or they might use pretend money to demonstrate the exchange. It might be that literacy support is required, so the teacher reads through the question again with the student and then asks them to explain, in their own words, the scenario being depicted, or uses picture cards to illustrate the events.

It might be that the transfer from wording to operation presents the greatest difficulty for the student, so they may provide some scaffolding by suggesting part of the information. This might include additional scaffolding, such as the question: 'We know we have less money at the end. Which operations mean that the answer will be smaller than the original amount?' The student may already know that subtraction and division result in smaller amounts, and then may be able to see where they might be applied with some further supportive questioning.

We can see that this is a responsive process that feeds into one of our key principles: know your students.

Proactive scaffolding, particularly during your training year and your NQT/RQT years, will involve you thinking about these choices at the lesson planning stage in some detail. This process will of course continue in later stages of your career, but you should give it your full attention during the early years, as this skill is absolutely paramount for highly effective teaching. Using our example above, it is easy to see how an informed and vigilant teacher might anticipate some of the needs outlined and prepare some scaffolding in advance, such as pictorial representations, or a box of money, or operations cards.

STRATEGIES FOR SUCCESS

This is the section in which we look at how you might make use of information to support your teaching. Following that, we consider some additional strategies that support the focus of this chapter.

GATHER YOUR INFORMATION

We have seen in this chapter that adaptive teaching requires a rounded understanding of the needs of your students. This will not happen by accident, or simply as a result of teaching your classes over time, although it will obviously help. You will need to be proactive and systematic if you are really going to understand the range and complexity of these needs. The more you can do this, the more effective you will be in the classroom, and outside it.

In order to really understand our students, we need to build a rounded picture. Adapting effectively, as we have seen, will be more effective if we understand the person as well as the learner. This means seeking out information in a proactive way. First, try to get to know your students as people as well as learners. Take the time to speak to students whenever you can. You can do this at the beginning and ending of lessons; you can make time for informal chat during lessons without impacting on the pace of learning too adversely; you can chat in the corridor; lunch duties and break duties create the ideal opportunity for talking to students; being available for some of your lunch, breaks and after school provides opportunities for students to speak in a more relaxed manner, as does running clubs, participating in trips, running events, or even just standing in the canteen queue. Everything that you learn about a student can be brought to bear effectively in supporting them as a learner. Take the time to ask them questions that inform your understanding. Questions might cover what they enjoy in lessons, things they find really difficult or activities they don't enjoy.

Consider next the people surrounding a student – their support network. Parents can be a huge help. A teacher showing an interest in their child's learning is nearly always met with positivity, and we just don't do it enough. Rather than merely relying on parents' evenings, aim to speak to parents as regularly as you can. A phone call to communicate a success will have a really positive impact and provides an opportunity for you to gain parental insight into a whole range of factors affecting learning. Keeping a record of such interactions and your learning from them will inform your planning. Form tutors in secondary schools usually know a great deal about their tutees. Take the time to speak to them and learn what you can – a staffroom chat over coffee can be very enlightening!

In addition, make use of the data on the system. Look at their reports: where are their strengths and areas for development? Look at the subjects in which they are progressing really well and seek out those teachers: how is this success being achieved? Do they have any additional needs? How are these needs recorded and has the school prepared any guidance on how they might be met? Build a profile of your students and find a means of recording this information so that it can inform your planning. Know your students – teach them as individuals.

TIPS FOR EFFECTIVE ADAPTATION

Let us now have a look at some tips for effective adaptation.

PLAN YOUR QUESTIONING

- Prepare questions for different stages of the lesson, using the three-tier-thinking model.

REVIEW THE LESSON CONSTANTLY

- Who is progressing well? Who needs support? Be systematic in your circulation and build a coherent picture.

(Continued)

ADAPT FOR POTENTIAL, NOT ABILITY

- Provide equity of opportunity for all. Don't limit somebody's learning as a result of placing a limit on their capabilities.

EXTEND YOUR RANGE OF DIFFERENTIATION STRATEGIES

- Look to adapt by pace, task, support, scaffold, instruction, explanation, question, choice, strength, responsibility and grouping. Remember, these can be blended.

AIM FOR MORE REACTIVE ADAPTATION

- While there is a role for proactive differentiation, we should be primarily looking to adapt as the need arises. Such adaptation will support your workload and ensure that false limits to learning don't arise.

BUILD A PROFILE OF YOUR STUDENTS

- Know their learning strengths in detail, and learn to anticipate when adaptation will be needed.

SUMMARY

In this chapter, we have covered:

- There is a moral and pragmatic imperative to adapt our teaching to meet the needs of the students – we simply cannot just teach the room. Achievement, engagement and well-being are all increased by taking the time to understand students and their needs. Know your students.
- If we adapt for our perception of a student's ability, we create an artificial ceiling on their achievement. We adapt for potential by offering scope for meaningful progress rather than offering tasks, resources or instruction that limit or reduce the progress a student might make.

- There are two types of adaptation. We can anticipate needs that might arise when we plan our lessons, based on sound knowledge of our students and their progress – this is proactive adaptation. During the lesson, we must stay alert to progress and learning needs as they arise, being prepared to step in with support wherever it is required – this is reactive adaptation.
- There is a huge range of strategies that we might employ. To use them effectively, we must develop our understanding of specific learning difficulties, social obstacles, cognitive capacity, memory and other conditions that affect learning.

REFERENCES

Alexander, J. (2020) *A Dialogic Teaching Companion*. London Routledge.

Binet, A., & Simon, T. (1905) New methods for diagnosis of the intellectual level of subnormals. *L'Annee Psychologique*, 14, 1–90.

Department for Education (2011) *Teachers' Standards*. London: HMSO. Accessed online (23 February 2021) at: www.gov.uk/government/publications/teachers-standards

Department for Education (2019) *ITT Core Content Framework*. London: HMSO. Accessed online (23 February 2021) at: www.gov.uk/government/publications/initial-teacher-training-itt-core-content-framework

Dewey, J. (1916/2011) *Democracy and Education: An Introduction to the Philosophy of Education*. New York: Simon and Brown.

Didau, D. (2019) *Making Kids Cleverer: A Manifesto for Closing the Advantage Gap*. Carmarthen: Crown House Publishing.

Dweck, C. (2006) *Mindset: How You Can Fulfil Your Potential*. London: Constable & Robinson.

Gardner, H. (2011) *Frames of Mind: The Theory of Multiple Intelligences*. London: Hachette.

Gregory, R. J. (1992) *Psychological Testing: History, Principles and Application*. Boston, MA: Allyn and Bacon.

Hirsch, E. D. (2016) *Why Knowledge Matters*. Cambridge, MA: Harvard University Press.

Honey, P., & Mumford, A. (1982) *Manual of Learning Styles*. London: P. Honey.

Lemov, D. (2010) *Teach like a Champion*. San Francisco, CA: Jossey-Bass.

Lucas, B., & Claxton, G. (2010) *New Kinds of Smart: How the Science of Learnable Intelligence is Changing Education*. Maidenhead: Open University Press.

Lucas, B., Claxton, G., & Spencer, E. (2013) *Expansive Education: Teaching Learners for the Real World*. Maidenhead: Open University Press.

Nancekivell, S., Shah, P., & Gelman, S. A. (2019) Maybe they're born with it, or maybe it's experience: Toward a deeper understanding of the learning style myth. *Journal of Educational Psychology*, 112(2), 221–235.

Spearman, C. (1927) *The Abilities of Man: Their Nature and Measurement.* London: Macmillan.

Sternberg, R. J. (1999) Looking back and looking forward on intelligence: Toward a theory of successful intelligence. In M. Bennett (ed.), *Developmental Psychology: Achievements and Prospects.* Philadelphia, PA: Psychology Press.

Vygotsky, L. (1934) *Thought and Language.* Cambridge, MA: MIT Press.

7

ASSESSMENT

INTRODUCTION

Assessment is a key skill in a teacher's repertoire. As well as making use of assessment in the classroom, teachers are held to account by the outcomes of assessments, as are schools. These two processes, while connected, are quite distinct from each other in nature. In this chapter, we will explore how they are connected and consider the impact for you as an early career teacher.

We will begin by looking at the role of external assessment (formal exams and tests) within the system. This will begin with a discussion concerning who is assessed and when, and with what degree of frequency. We will then consider how the information from these assessments impacts on schools, referring to both Ofsted outcomes and the impact on community reputation. Understanding the impacts will help you to rationalise your place as an individual teacher within the accountability system.

Next, we look at the different forms of assessment and their impact on classroom practice. Two key forms of assessment, formative and summative, will be analysed in detail, with a close focus on their application in the classroom. We will also look at the role of feedback, self and peer assessment and retrieval practice. To conclude, we will analyse some key strategies that you might employ to ensure that assessment has a purposeful role in your teaching.

THE *TEACHING STANDARDS* AND THE *CORE CONTENT FRAMEWORK*

Teachers' Standard 6 is focused on assessment. It outlines the following expectations:

Make accurate and productive use of assessment:

- know and understand how to assess the relevant subject and curriculum areas, including statutory assessment requirements
- make use of formative and summative assessment to secure students' progress
- use relevant data to monitor progress, set targets, and plan subsequent lessons
- give students regular feedback, both orally and through accurate marking, and encourage students to respond to the feedback (Department for Education, 2011)

The *Core Content Framework* outlines the following key areas of knowledge:

1. Effective assessment is critical to teaching because it provides teachers with information about students' understanding and needs.
2. Good assessment helps teachers avoid being over-influenced by potentially misleading factors, such as how busy students appear.

3. Before using any assessment, teachers should be clear about the decision it will be used to support and be able to justify its use.
4. To be of value, teachers use information from assessments to inform the decisions they make; in turn, students must be able to act on feedback for it to have an effect.
5. High-quality feedback can be written or verbal; it is likely to be accurate and clear, encourage further effort, and provide specific guidance on how to improve.
6. Over time, feedback should support students to monitor and regulate their own learning.
7. Working with colleagues to identify efficient approaches to assessment is important; assessment can become onerous and have a disproportionate impact on workload. (Department for Education, 2019)

Each of these key 'learn that' statements will be explored through this chapter and we will flag them up at the point at which they become relevant.

THE ROLE OF EXTERNAL ASSESSMENT

Students are generally assessed at the end of Key Stages, although there are exceptions. In primary schools, this is at the end of Key Stage 1 (Year 2) and Key Stage 2 (Year 6). The Key Stage 2 assessments are particularly critical within the system as a whole. They are used to determine the success of the students' primary education and, concurrently, the success of the schools they attend.

The Key Stage 2 tests comprise a sequence of formal tests that are taken in school and then marked externally. The tests comprise a grammar test, a reading and comprehension test, spelling tests, an arithmetic test and a maths reasoning test. They are a key focus of effort for primary schools. So much so, in fact, that the bulk of curriculum time has been devoted to increasing the literacy and numeracy skills needed to pass them. However, we are seeing a change in emphasis now, as Ofsted's key focus is breadth and depth within the curriculum. This creates a challenging tension for primary leaders and teachers as they seek to find a balance, while providing quality teaching and learning.

The results of the Key Stage 2 test are compared with those from Key Stage 1 and a progress score is calculated, which is then compared with national averages for similar students. The outcomes from these tests are reported on the school performance tables and form a key evaluation tool for Ofsted inspectors.

The outcomes from these tests are also important for secondary schools (and obviously, the young people who have to sit them). The Department for Education uses these tests to calculate expected outcomes for students at the end of Key Stage 4 (Year 11), which are then communicated to schools. Secondary schools are measured on how well their students perform in relation to those expectations. This is called a Progress 8 score, which is a quite simple (some think much too simple) calculation based on comparing the expectation with the outcome. As a result, most secondary schools employ target-setting systems that have some relationship with those expectations. Again, the outcomes from GCSE examinations, including the Progress 8 score, are made public via the performance tables. They are also used by inspectors arriving at their judgements. All of this information is available to parents when they make their choice of school.

ASSESSMENT, ACCOUNTABILITY AND SCHOOL SUCCESS

All of this information is of value to you as you begin your training. You will quickly realise that schools are accountability-driven institutions, and that, consequently, the role of a teacher is subject to monitoring, assessment and scrutiny, both from within the school itself, but also from external partners, including parents, the Department for Education and inspection bodies.

Arising from this accountability structure, expectations will be communicated to you about eventual student outcomes. When students are not on track to achieve their outcomes, you will be expected to demonstrate the steps that you have taken to support them in getting there. Your exam or test outcomes, in particular, will be evaluated and monitored.

This is because the outcomes achieved by your students will form part of the wider picture of the school's progress. There is an important point to make at this stage. The results belong to the students, not the school. We can forget, within a framework of data analysis, target setting and accountability, that what really matters is the young people, their learning, their success, their development and their achievements.

Having said that, for most leaders in schools, student success is synchronous with the success of the school itself and is therefore part of a complementary discourse in which student success, school success, numbers on roll, local reputation, inspection success and ongoing improvement all conflate to mean one thing: the school, its staff and its leaders are effective. This is critically important, because since the Education Reform Act 1988, parents and carers have a choice about which school they attend. Schools are working in a marketplace in which they have to attract customers. It is a complex framework within which to operate. Bad results can mean a poor inspection outcome. A poor inspection and bad results impact on reputation. Reputational damage means fewer parents choose the school, which means a reduction in income and thus further potential impact. Recruitment of teaching staff can also be affected and, eventually, a school can find itself in significant existential difficulty, at which point, Department for Education intervention is likely, including a change of leadership and possibly even school identity.

REFLECTIVE QUESTION

- Look up a school that you know on the school performance tables. What information is included there? Does it reflect your knowledge of the school?

Schools are consequently looking for teachers with a high level of subject and curriculum expertise. Therefore, understanding assessment frameworks, the knowledge and skills that they require of students and the pedagogy best suited to delivering those will be a critical part of your role in school. There are many exam specifications in the secondary sector (all built from the same framework). Before you begin teaching in school, make sure that you have some familiarity with the specification being used (secondary) and the content of the tests at Key Stages 1 and 2 (primary).

The expectation that teachers achieve results, meet targets and provide the very best for students is high. Rightly so, you might think. Sadly, some schools don't always communicate this in the best manner and it can result in stressed teachers and stressed students. You can only do your best and nobody can ask any more of you than that. If you plan for the individuals in your groups, pay attention to their individual progress and build your understanding in the manner this book recommends, you will be on the path towards meeting those accountability expectations.

ASSESSMENT AND THE CLASSROOM

Assessment can be employed to improve the learning in your classroom. Trainees that I work with are asked to identify, in their planning, how it will be used at each stage of the lesson. This may sound surprising. Does it mean that they are conducting assessments every 10 minutes? The answer is yes, and no.

Assessment can be thought of as falling (broadly) into two categories: summative and formative. *Summative assessment* is essentially testing, or the assessment *of* learning. Its purpose is to ascertain what knowledge, skills or understanding have been gained within a period of time. We might also attribute a grade to that, essentially rating the level of success in those achievements. *Formative assessment* can be thought of as assessment *for* learning. It is a group of processes that take place in the classroom, the purpose of which is to ascertain current progress in understanding in relation to what is being taught. This then results in an immediate teacher response; teaching is adapted as a result of what is learned during the formative process and/or feedback is provided to students.

We are going to focus in the main on formative assessment in this chapter, as this is the key skill that you will need to develop in order to meet the standards, but summative assessment does have a role in this: summative assessments can be used formatively. Any information that you have in relation to achievement is useful, as we have seen in the 'Gather your information' sections of this book. You can access prior attainment data about your students quite easily in most schools. It's particularly useful when picking up a new class. Making use of this information in your planning will lead to better learning, as we see in the sub-standard:

> Use relevant data to monitor progress, set targets, and plan subsequent lessons.
> (Department for Education, 2011)

Formative assessment has been part of education dialogue since the 1960s, but it was in the 1990s that it really gained traction as a fundamental element of practice. This was thanks to the breakthrough work undertaken by Paul Black and Dylan Wiliam, two academics from the University of London. Their significant work, 'Inside the black box' (Black & Wiliam, 1998a) and accompanying papers, broke new ground in developing our understanding of how assessment might be applied in the classroom. They reviewed a huge range of studies (Black & Wiliam, 1998b) and found that classrooms that made use of formative approaches enjoyed a typical effect size ranging from 0.4–0.7. These findings are supported by Hattie (2012: 266), whose meta-analysis gave the following effect sizes: formative evaluation (0.90) and feedback (0.75).

How can we use these findings to refine our practice? The answer is that formative assessment must be integral at all stages of the lesson. It requires both careful planning and responsive flexibility during your lessons. As such, it means that this is a skill that you are likely to start refining at a later stage of your teacher training programme, but that doesn't mean you can't aim to use it from the start.

REFLECTIVE QUESTION

- What processes might you employ to discover how much pupils have learned during the course of a lesson?

Begin with your success criteria. Good planning, as we have seen, means being absolutely clear about the learning you are aiming for. Really good planning means that you are also clear about the success criteria for each stage of your lesson, and that you have planned for how you will check for this. Following this 'check on learning', teaching is responsive to what you ascertain about the learning. Figure 7.1 illustrates the cyclical nature of this process.

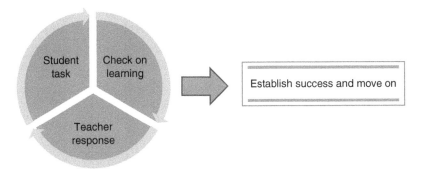

Figure 7.1 Responding to student learning

The first stage of the process is presented as a cycle because it can be used iteratively. It links very clearly to Rosenshines's (2010) concept of securing a high success rate. There is little point in continuing to the next stage of your lesson if you haven't secured the necessary knowledge and understanding needed to cope with it. The processes that accompany a task are just as important as the task itself. This is why formative assessment is so integral to effective practice. You are teaching the students, not the room; you are strengthening your knowledge of the students and you are forensically focused on their learning.

REFLECTIVE QUESTION

- What routines might a teacher employ to ensure that they have established both knowledge and understanding? Is there potential for these routines to disrupt the flow of the learning?

Let's have a look at how this works in an actual lesson setting. We begin with our objective. In this instance, we are going to use material from a Year 8 English lesson. Here is an objective from the lesson plan:

- We can apply our understanding of character and language to *select* and *justify* whether quotes suggest Prospero acts out of love for Miranda or hatred for others.

TASK

Related to the objective, the students are given a sliding scale with love at one end and hate at the other, as well as a group of carefully selected quotations from the play.

They must choose where to place the quotations on the scale and be prepared to explain their choices. The success criteria for the stage of the lesson are clearly articulated within the objective: are learners able to apply their knowledge of the text and characters in categorising the quotations?

CHECK ON LEARNING

Following the task, the plan is to use a questioning and feedback session to ascertain how students are progressing in relation to the objective. The aim is to target questions, carefully, across a range of students, taking account of anticipated progress. The questions we use at this stage can employ three-tier-thinking. It's worth noting at this point that this would also be a good example of adaptation and meeting individual needs. At this stage, the aim is to gather as much evidence as possible about the understanding and, more specifically, the gaps in that understanding, arising from the task.

TEACHER RESPONSE

Inevitably, a range of responses are offered by the students. Some are effective in providing justification for their responses, some less so. As a teacher, you might respond in a number of ways at this point. Table 7.1 provides some indication of the way in which you could work at this point. It is unlikely that you would use them all at once, although if time permits, you could.

Table 7.1 Teacher responses to checks on learning

Response 1	Immediate feedback, offered to the whole class, about successful responses. Students might be invited to identify the successful elements through discussion. Students might also discuss the successful strategies employed in arriving at these elements (metacognitive talk).
Response 2	Immediate feedback, sensitively and constructively articulated, about how less successful responses could be improved. Students might also contribute to this.
Response 3	Students consider their own work in light of the findings from the class feedback. What do they need to improve?
Response 4	If necessary, extra time might be given to complete the task in greater depth, based on increased understanding.
Response 5	Moving to the next task (writing about their selections) occurs once sufficient success is achieved. Feedback to the class at this stage is specific about what constitutes success in the task, and also about which processes are most likely to yield success (metacognitive talk). It is essentially a summary of the key learning.

| Response 6 | Based on the feedback, modelling the next task on the board, co-constructed with the students, built from a shared understanding of successful responses. |
| Response 7 | As students move on to the next task, findings from the checks on learning and the feedback process are used to target subsequent support that might be needed for individuals or groups. This may involve additional instruction/explanation, scaffolded resources, one-to-one support on strategy selection, further modelling, scaffolding through questions, personalised feedback, further checks on understanding or simply targeted progress checks. |

FEEDBACK

All of the above strategies will be referred to in more detail as we progress through the next sections of this chapter. Let's begin by looking at how to provide feedback effectively.

FEEDBACK AND CLASSROOM CULTURE

Before we look at some of the specific strategies involved in providing feedback to students, we need to consider the role of classroom culture in doing so. We saw in Chapter 3 on learning that 'mindsets' have a critical role to play. Students who are performance-oriented are less likely to respond well to challenging tasks than those who are mastery-oriented (Dweck, 2006).

The culture that you create in your classroom is critical here. Classrooms in which students respond negatively to feedback, either through negative emotional responses or simply not using it to improve their work, are classrooms where learning will be much harder to secure. We can see in Table 7.1 that feedback involves highlighting to students where mistakes have been made. It also involves engaging the class in looking for ways to manage processes differently. Students who are insecure, or who feel a lack of trust in the learning environment, will not be able to respond in the way that you need them to.

Fostering a growth mindset, or mastery-oriented approach, should form the core of classroom culture. An environment in which mistakes are positioned as learning opportunities, rather than a cause for dismay, is what you are aiming for. Mistakes are steps on the road to mastery.

REFLECTIVE QUESTION

- What could you say to a student to help them reframe a mistake as a learning opportunity?

The behaviour for learning that accompanies reframing of error should also be developed explicitly and should be centred on mutual respect. Don't allow expressions of derision in response to incorrect answers to go unchallenged. Ensure that when a student is sharing their thoughts, there is respectful silence. Encourage the language of constructive criticism: rather than 'that was wrong because...', support students in developing expressions like 'that could be improved by...' or 'they might also consider...' or 'they could try to...'. Encourage students to develop the skill of identifying developmental success in both outcome and process. Feedback from peers could include 'their work has really improved since yesterday because...' or 'the way they did that was really clever because...'.

This process won't come naturally to the students initially and will require you to be explicit in shaping how you want things to be done. Polite reminders, clearly articulated expectations and a firm but developmentally focused response to deliberate disruptions of this culture, over time, will see you achieve the learning process that you are looking for.

FEEDBACK TYPES

Table 7.1 illustrated a number of different ways in which you might configure feedback. In this section, we are delving into two statements from the *Core Content Framework* (CCF), as follows:

> To be of value, teachers use information from assessments to inform the decisions they make; in turn, students must be able to act on feedback for it to have an effect.
>
> High-quality feedback can be written or verbal; it is likely to be accurate and clear, encourage further effort, and provide specific guidance on how to improve. (Department for Education, 2019: 23)

Let's have a look at this in detail.

Response 1 is feedback based upon identifying successes and the process is collaborative. It is collaborative because the research shows that when you activate the students as instructors for each other, feedback is more effective (Leahy & Wiliam, 2009). Note that feedback on both outcomes and process is employed. In this type of feedback, you are aiming to be explicit about success criteria, which supports the students in positioning their work successfully. You are also looking to identify, through explicit metacognitive talk, the successful approaches employed in arriving at this point.

Response 2 is focused upon identifying where the outcomes have been less successful. Again, this is collaborative and will be the test of the learning culture you have created: can these mistakes be employed constructively to deepen student understanding in a manner that is mastery-oriented? Metacognitive talk features here also: how might the approach to the task be reconfigured to achieve greater success?

Both Response 1 and Response 2 employ feedback methodology that Hattie (2012: 133–134) describes as 'task and product level' feedback and 'process level' feedback. Task level refers in the main to accuracy, and process level to the means employed in arriving at the conclusion. He explains that both of these can be highly beneficial in developing student confidence and self-efficacy.

Make sure that when feeding back in this manner, students are given the opportunity to consider the implications for their own work, which is Response 3. An example of how to do this could be posing the question, then allowing a think–pair–share process in which students support each other's thought process.

Response 3, in turn, develops Hattie's third feedback level, which he describes as the 'self-regulation or conditional level' (Hattie, 2012: 134). At this point, students are developing the capacity to identify their own feedback as well as the value of practice, of trying again, of improvement, of tenacity and, most importantly, of taking ownership of their own development. This relates clearly to the CCF statement that:

> Over time, feedback should support students to monitor and regulate their own learning. (Department for Education, 2019: 23)

At this point, the students are employing both self-assessment and peer assessment. Such strategies are at their most successful when they are carefully directed, employ specific, identifiable success criteria, and are mastery-oriented rather than performance-oriented. Simply put, if you just ask students to mark each other's work, or their own work, the learning outcomes will be negligible. Establish exactly what you want them to look for, base it firmly on the learning you have explicitly signposted, and don't ask them to grade it. They are looking for developmental opportunities and key areas of success.

Response 4 may or may not be needed, depending on what you discover in the check on learning. Don't be afraid to take the time you need to secure the learning. Be prepared to explain things again, explain them differently, ask questions and probe for understanding and then give them the opportunity to take the time to consolidate the understanding they need in order to progress.

Response 5 is the point at which you establish the key messages. Summarise, succinctly, the important learning from the feedback process. Be careful not to create cognitive overload at this point. It's easy to create a long list of micro-improvements, but they won't be able to work to all of these instantaneously. Tease out the important points, summarise them succinctly and then give them opportunity to apply them. This is further consolidated through Response 6, in which you work with the students to construct a model answer that demonstrates these findings.

Response 7 is the point at which you can use feedback as an adaptive strategy alongside other supportive measures. As you run the formative process, continue to pay very close attention to the evidence that students provide in their response. Who is likely to need further help? Make notes (you can't remember it all) as you work through your response process and then, once the students are working independently, look to effectively prioritise. Who needs the most immediate help? Can a small group be assisted in the same manner? If you're lucky enough to have a teaching assistant (TA), how might they be deployed in providing the support that is needed?

Trying out some of these strategies will support you in understanding the learning in the room. Tom Sherrington (2019) has identified teachers' failure to understand the learning as the 'Number 1 problem' in teaching. He's right. He presents a number of solutions and identifies much of what we have discussed here. A key expectation he articulates is to aim for 'all knowing all', as opposed to just checking if one or two can demonstrate the learning. It's a robust challenge to us all and should provide a framework for our questioning, our feedback, our formative assessment practices and our next steps.

WRITTEN FEEDBACK

Written feedback, or marking, has evolved considerably in recent years. This is mainly the result of workload reform, as marking students' work, alongside data inputting, can be really onerous. This is usually the result of unreasonable or poorly conceived expectations as leaders seek to meet the demands of external frameworks. Thankfully, thinking has shifted. The focus is now on quality and the impact on learning, rather than demonstrating that books have been marked on a regular basis. You will be expected to follow a departmental or school policy in relation to marking, but there may also be an element of flexibility with regards to frequency, amount and nature of feedback.

Written feedback should follow the same principles as verbal feedback, but there are some differences in the way that it might be applied, and this provides you with some distinct opportunities to respond to individual progress, offer corrective advice and, most importantly of all, for the student to act on this.

Written feedback is at its most useful when it is diagnostic (it identifies the areas for development) and dialogic (it poses questions that prompt the student to think further). If you structure it in this manner, the feedback will be formative (Marshall & Wiliam, 2006).

Let's consider some examples. In the example below, the teacher has responded to a Year 9 biology assessment in which the student has written an extended answer about Darwin's theory of evolution, explaining how he identified that organisms change over time.

> This is mostly well written. You have explained your ideas clearly and show some understanding of the theory and how Darwin arrived at it. Your SPaG is erratic. There are some inaccuracies at points, so you need to read the theory again and make sure that you understand it. You also need to write a bit more and make a bit more effort.

If you look at this example, it's hard to see how the student might make use of the feedback to secure improvement. Where are the errors? They might not know what erratic means. Is reading the theory likely to improve their understanding? Write a bit more about what, exactly? It is simply a generic summary with a generous dose of judgement, and not what a student needs to improve.

Let's consider a more focused response, designed to support the student in securing improvement:

> Well done on some good content, although there are some areas that you need to improve. You have effectively explained how Darwin accounted for change over time in organisms, but there is a gap. While you have included environmental change, you might also have explained how 'inherited variation' works. What did Darwin say about this? You have explained that organisms are classified, but could you provide an example of how this works? When you finish, proof-read your work, as there are some spelling errors (I have highlighted some for you).

The second piece of written feedback is actionable. It is diagnostic in that it provides specific areas of success, but also identifies specific gaps. It is dialogic in that it has posed some further questions for the student to consider. In this feedback, the teacher also indicates that there is in-text notation. The feedback will be even more useful if the teacher identifies specifically where the gaps are, in the margin or within the text.

The key to making the marking process meaningful is to provide an opportunity for students to respond. When the work is returned to the students, make time, ideally at the beginning of a lesson, for them to respond in writing and improve their work. If you don't do this, they may read it and then forget about it, or they may not even read it!

RETRIEVAL PRACTICE

Retrieval practice is included in this chapter as it can be employed for the purposes of formative assessment, as well as employing assessment methodology to boost student recall over time. It is not, however, a form of assessment in itself, and applying it in such a manner is likely to be detrimental. It is a learning activity, first and foremost, but it is easy to see how the information a teacher gains from such a process could inform teaching and learning in subsequent lessons.

Essentially, retrieval practice involves building memory-boosting exercises into your lessons in a systematic manner. These exercises require students to recall something that they have learnt in the past. Reviewing material through retrieval practice strategies supports and develops long-term memory (Roediger & Karpicke, 2006). It compensates for the 'forgetting curve' developed by Ebbinghaus (1880) in the 19th century, which demonstrated the rate at which we forget information if we don't access it again. As we saw in Chapter 3 on learning, Rosenshine (2010) recommends a process of daily, weekly and monthly review that employs such strategies.

There is a caveat to this. Retrieval practice is not simply conducting endless assessments so that you can check what your students have learnt. Working in such a manner is detrimental to student well-being as it will create stressful, performance-oriented situations. It is also not intended to increase your own workload by creating additional, unnecessary marking. The process should be about students checking on their own knowledge, identifying their own gaps and working to improve on these, over time. If you work in this manner, it can actually reduce their stress (as they gain in knowledge and confidence), and provide them with the necessary skillset to revise effectively.

Retrieval practice can be delivered through 'low stakes' testing. By 'low stakes', we mean that the tests are not used to grade, categorise or generate data. The impact on the students should be to support a mastery-oriented rather than a performance-oriented approach. This is the opposite of tense, silent and high-stakes testing in which students feel measured, scrutinised and pressurised. Ideally, the experience for the students should be formative and reassuring. They test their own knowledge, identify their strengths and gaps, improve their recall and gain in confidence.

Retrieval practice is at its most effective when 'desirable difficulty' is built in (Bjork, 1994). The work should contain just enough challenge to place the students at the point at which they are stretched. The evidence suggests that this is the point at which the long-term benefit for students is increased. In the short term, they will find this challenging at first (you want them to). Working together, you can build their resilience over time and develop their capacity for embracing challenge as they realise that the process is improving their knowledge and understanding.

It works best when you employ the techniques of spacing and interleaving. *Spacing* means returning to the same subject matter in short bursts, rather than trying to slog through it all in one huge effort. Simply put, you might run a short quiz on the same topic over a sequence of days, rather than conducting a three-hour revision session that tries to do it all at once. *Interleaving* is the skill of weaving together related (but different) domain-specific material so that students form stronger schema. It allows students to make connections between connected subjects and strengthen understanding. In retrieval practice, this would mean the careful selection of recall material that forms a connection with the main body of learning in the lesson.

Retrieval practice strategies could include:

- A quiz at the beginning of the lesson – on the board, on paper, the teacher reading out questions or the students testing each other
- Labelling diagrams
- Summarising – creating key headings for a process
- Listing

- Speaking with authority – students talk without stopping for one minute on specified topics. They get points for mentioning key words
- Completing a knowledge organiser, such as a fishbone diagram
- Students modelling a process, routine or procedure for their peers, in pairs or small groups
- Telling the story – students narrate an event, a cause and effect, a scientific process, etc., in pairs, small groups or individually
- Creating a mindmap of a topic area
- Students creating flashcards on topics and then quizzing each other using the cards as prompts

There are lots of other techniques that you might employ. Kate Jones (2021) has developed some excellent resources if you would like to explore these strategies further.

STRATEGIES FOR SUCCESS

This is the section in which we look at how you might make use of information to support your teaching. Following that, we consider some additional strategies that support the focus of this chapter.

GATHER YOUR INFORMATION

BEFORE THE LESSON

Make use of data relating to the students. This is a key requirement of the *Teachers' Standards*, as we have seen earlier in this chapter. You can access data related to their achievement in school reports (primary and secondary), departmental data (secondary) and from existing or previous teachers' records. Use this information to identify potential gaps, to create groups and to plan where to start your targeted support and/or adaptations. Triangulate what you find by talking to teachers who know the students – do their views support what you have found? You can also access information related to SEND and assess the likely impact in your planned learning. Some schools use information systems that allow you to arrange seating plans. If they are available, make use of them. Build this information into your planning to ensure greater success, particularly when you first meet a class.

DURING THE LESSON

Make formative assessment a core, integrated element of your practice. This is not just an add-on, or a requirement of trainees' lesson plans. It is absolutely fundamental. Simply

(Continued)

put, it is the difference between an average teacher and a really effective one. Remain vigilant throughout the lesson: make it your aim to discover as much as you can about what the students have learned and develop the skill of modifying teaching in response to what you have discovered. A responsive, watchful approach is based upon paying attention to the learning and supporting students with really effective feedback on their progress.

AFTER THE LESSON

Reflect, and be diligent in doing so. While the lesson is still fresh in your mind, ask yourself some key assessment questions. Who learnt what today? How do I know what they learnt? What evidence was there of the learning? Make notes about students. What are the implications for the next lesson? What adaptations will be necessary? At what point will I create retrieval opportunities, and upon what elements of the learning will I focus these retrieval opportunities? How effective were my checks on learning and did my feedback have a tangible impact on learning?

TIPS FOR EFFECTIVE USE OF ASSESSMENT

PAY ATTENTION TO THE LEARNING AT ALL STAGES OF THE LESSON

- Know your students. It is the learning that matters and remember to teach them as individuals.

PLAN YOUR QUESTIONS FOR EACH STAGE OF THE LESSON

- Use the three-tier-thinking model to map your assessment questions at key stages of the lesson.

USE ASSESSMENT TO CHECK IF YOU HAVE ESTABLISHED SUCCESS IN YOUR LEARNING OBJECTIVES

- There is little point in moving to the next stage if you have not secured the understanding required to access it.

PERSONAL WHITEBOARDS ARE A QUICK WAY OF GAUGING UNDERSTANDING

- Students can write quickly on personal whiteboards to produce a sentence, summarise an idea, display their working and solution or to draw quick diagrams.

DEVELOP A SYSTEM FOR CHECKING ON LEARNING

- Whom will you check on, when, and with what frequency? Keep a record and ensure that all students are given the opportunities and support they need.

ESTABLISH, AND COMMUNICATE EXPLICITLY, THE SUCCESS CRITERIA FOR EACH STAGE OF THE LESSON

- Use the three-tier-thinking model to identify and articulate your objectives. Keep these live throughout the lesson by reminding students about them and framing your questions in relation to them.

MEANINGFUL, DIALOGIC APPROACHES TO CLASSROOM TALK WILL BOTH DEEPEN UNDERSTANDING AND PROVIDE FORMATIVE ASSESSMENT OPPORTUNITIES

- Look to pose questions that foster debate, expand upon answers, consider different viewpoints, test ideas and tackle problems. Listen carefully as you do so – to learn about your students.

PRIOR ATTAINMENT DATA, COUPLED WITH STUDENT INFORMATION, WILL ENABLE YOU TO PLAN FOR YOUR STUDENTS MORE EFFECTIVELY

- Access the available information and use it to consider the needs of both the group and the individual students.

DON'T CONFUSE 'WORK' FOR LEARNING

- When you circulate, actually look to see what has been produced, rather than looking to see if something has been produced.

SEEK OPPORTUNITIES TO ENGAGE THE STUDENTS IN MEANINGFUL PEER AND SELF-ASSESSMENT

- Provide the information that they need to do this effectively. The evidence supports its efficacy if the peer and self-assessment is done supportively and rigorously.

(Continued)

QUALITY FEEDBACK IS EXPLICIT AND SPECIFIC ABOUT THE NEXT STEPS FOR STUDENTS

- Feedback that identifies exactly how to improve or develop the work will secure progress in learning.

IF YOU PROVIDE FEEDBACK, CREATE THE TIME TO RESPOND TO IT

- Feedback without an opportunity to respond to it is just feedback without impact – it is not an effective use of your time.

A CLASSROOM CULTURE IN WHICH MISTAKES ARE SEEN AS DEVELOPMENTAL OPPORTUNITIES ENCOURAGES LEARNING

- Be explicit about the rules and expectations when sharing thoughts and/or sharing work. A safe environment, built on mutual respect, enhances formative assessment processes.

SUMMARY

In this chapter, we have covered:

- Assessment is a broad term that can be applied to a variety of processes. It is an information-gathering tool, part of an accountability framework and a valuable skill that teachers can apply in the classroom.
- Schools are subject to high levels of external accountability, which is based in part on the outcomes of assessments. It means that the role and performance of a teacher is accountable as well. As a consequence, schools are environments in which account-ability is a key driver in processes and decision-making.
- Students are assessed throughout their education. These assessments form key 'gateways' and can have an impact on target setting and school progress scores.
- Assessment can be thought of as either summative or formative. Summative assess-ments are used to capture progress and attainment at key points in the curriculum. Formative assessment is the process of gauging student learning and then responding, either

through feedback on next steps, or by modifying teaching in response. Summative assessments can also be used formatively.

- Formative assessment is a core skill for effective teaching. It is not an add-on or complementary process. If you use it as a key tool, consistently deployed throughout lessons, it will enable you to gauge the learning effectively, and subsequently identify gaps, misconceptions and successes. It places the focus on the learning, not the teaching, and facilitates the process of getting to know your students so that you can support them as individuals.

REFERENCES

Bjork, R. A. (1994) Institutional impediments to effective training. In D. Druckman & R. A. Bjork (eds), *Learning, Remembering, Believing: Enhancing Human Performance*. Washington, DC: National Academy Press.

Black, P., & Wiliam, D. (1998a) Inside the black box: Raising standards through classroom assessment. *Phi Delta Kappan*, 80(2), 139–148.

Black, P., & Wiliam, D. (1998b) Assessment and classroom learning. *Assessment in Education, Principles, Policy and Practice*, 5(1), 7–74.

Department for Education (2011) *Teachers' Standards*. London: HMSO. Accessed online (23 February 2021) at: www.gov.uk/government/publications/teachers-standards

Department for Education (2019) *ITT Core Content Framework*. London: HMSO. Accessed online (23 February 2021) at: www.gov.uk/government/publications/initial-teacher-training-itt-core-content-framework

Dweck, C. S. (2006) *Mindset: How You Can Fulfil Your Potential*. New York: Random House.

Ebbinghaus, H. (1880) Urmanuskript "Ueber das Gedächtniß". Passau: Passavia Universitätsverlag.

Education Reform Act 1988. London: HMSO. Accessed online (23 February 2021) at: www.legislation.gov.uk/ukpga/1988/40/contents

Hattie, J. (2012) *Visible Learning for Teachers: Maximising Impact on Learning*. Abingdon: Routledge.

Jones, K. (2021) *Retrieval Practice: Resource Guide: Ideas and Activities for the Classroom*. Woodbridge: John Catt Educational.

Leahy, S., & Wiliam, D. (2009) *Embedding Assessment for Learning: A Professional Development Pack*. London: Specialist Schools and Academies Trust.

Marshall, L., & Wiliam, D. (2006) *Inside the Black Box: Assessment and Learning in the English Classroom*. Oxford: NFER Nelson.

Roediger, H. L., & Karpicke, J. D. (2006) Test-enhanced learning: Taking memory tests improves long-term retention. *Psychological Science*, 17(3), 249–255.

Rosenshine, B. (2010) Principles of Instruction. The International Academy of Education (IAE) *Educational Practices* Series 21. London: IAE.

Sherrington, T. (2019) The #1 problem/weakness in teaching and how to address it. *teacherhead* [Blog]. Posted 4 October 2019. Accessed online (7 June 2021) at: The #1 problem/weakness in teaching and how to address it. | teacherhead

8

CLASSROOM MANAGEMENT

INTRODUCTION

If you help us to learn, we will help you to teach.

Samuel, Year 11, Leeds

Samuel is right. Remember his point as we progress through this chapter – behaviour is reciprocal. Speak to anybody about entering the profession and the likelihood is that their first comment will be related to classroom management. The majority of the public will balk at the idea of managing 30 5-year-olds or teenagers. This is understandable, it's a daunting prospect. Applicants for training usually cite classroom management as their biggest concern during interview. However, if you remember the guiding principles of 'know your students' and 'teach the students, not the room', it is entirely achievable.

In effect, good behaviour from your students should be the product of following the tips at the end of each chapter in this book. It is the product of refined practice that is centred on learning, excellent relationships, clear expectations and a carefully established culture of mutual respect. The first thing to understand is that the implementation and maintenance of a well-behaved classroom depends upon the engagement of the students. Effective planning for structured learning, supported by well-prepared resources, is the absolute bedrock of good behaviour. The means by which to achieve it are covered in other chapters in this book. Capitalising on the relationship between these other tips and the strategies covered in this chapter will, in time, deliver the practised finesse you are looking for. Consequently, looking at behaviour in isolation needs to be approached with caution, as it simply doesn't work in this way.

Having said that, there are a number of strategies and principles that you can employ to foster attentive behaviour. In this chapter, we will begin by looking at the link between relationships and authority. This then links to the idea of classroom culture and how a teacher establishes expectations. We will then explore how to establish rules, the role of consistency and the concept of tolerance within that. Following that, we take a close look at establishing a healthy balance in your range of responses and conclude by considering the role of self-regulation in establishing a credible teacher persona.

REFLECTIVE QUESTION

- Consider the relationship between engagement and behaviour. Is it possible to ensure good behaviour from students who are disinterested in the learning?

THE TEACHERS' STANDARDS, ENGAGEMENT AND BEHAVIOUR

Training and qualifying to teach is a process that requires you to demonstrate that you can create an ordered and productive learning environment. The *Teachers' Standards* describe this as follows:

1. Set high expectations which inspire, motivate and challenge students

   - establish a safe and stimulating environment for students, rooted in mutual respect
   - set goals that stretch and challenge students of all backgrounds, abilities and dispositions
   - demonstrate consistently the positive attitudes, values and behaviour which are expected of students
2. Manage behaviour effectively to ensure a good and safe learning environment

   - have clear rules and routines for behaviour in classrooms, and take responsibility for promoting good and courteous behaviour both in classrooms and around the school, in accordance with the school's behaviour policy
   - have high expectations of behaviour, and establish a framework for discipline with a range of strategies, using praise, sanctions and rewards consistently and fairly
   - manage classes effectively, using approaches which are appropriate to students' needs in order to involve and motivate them
   - maintain good relationships with students, exercise appropriate authority, and act decisively when necessary. (Department for Education, 2011)

A careful read of these standards (and the rest of them) will find more than an echo of our guiding principles. The focus is on the individual, on relationships and on respect. This is echoed in the *ITT Core Content Framework*, where the 'Learn that' statements are organised by standard (Department for Education, 2019).

There is one very important point to be made right at the outset. Positive working relationships are essential in modern education. Gone are the days when the schoolmaster could rule by fear, assaulting students at will and imposing dreadful and humiliating punishments – and rightly so. Gone also are the students who enter classrooms filled with automatic respect for their elders and betters (if ever this was the case).

The modern teacher has to establish, build and nurture mutual respect. Forget what you have been told about not smiling, setting examples and other such anachronistic advice; they are not effective. Instead, think about who you want to be and who you want your students to be when they are in your teaching space. This has a relationship with our guiding principles. Certainly, 'know your students' has a role to play here.

Additionally, balancing the positive and the negative is key. Many people struggle with this concept on entering the profession. How to be authoritarian and still build relationships? How to 'win them over' and still maintain order? Invariably, the classrooms in which disorder is prevalent are the ones in which the teacher has failed to strike this balance. Be reassured though, it's not a matter of absolute fine-tuning. The margin for error is vast – most situations can be recovered: *most*.

RELATIONSHIPS AND AUTHORITY

A culture of mutual trust and respect supports effective relationships. (Department for Education, 2019: 9)

The above 'Learn that' statement from the *Core Content Framework* is critical to understanding how authority works in a classroom. Authority is not automatic, simply because you are standing at the front of the room in role as a teacher. Authority arises from respect. Respect in the classroom is achieved by treating others respectfully, fairly and consistently, and by being effective in your role – this establishes trust. Good classroom relationships are partly determined by this dynamic. When you watch an experienced teacher expertly managing a group of students, what you are seeing is the product of carefully established routines, rules, expectations and relationships. It will have taken time to embed and there will have been several hiccups along the way. Trust and respect take time to establish and they have to be worked at.

When we use the word 'authority' in a teaching context, it is not helpful to connote that we are enforcers, deliverers of the law, or that we are beyond reproach. Having said that, when you step in front of a class, you need to communicate that you are in charge, that you are the owner of the space and its norms, systems and interactions. The aim is to be comfortably in charge, while communicating to your students that you care deeply about their progress, their learning and their well-being. If your students understand that your operating principles are grounded in this ethos, and they see that you are successful in delivery, they will support you.

Confidence has a large part to play in creating this environment. You will inevitably be nervous when you first go into schools, and even more so when you first lead a lesson. Accept that confidence takes some time to build and that it will be the result of a process of trial and error. You will make mistakes, but you will also experience successes. Both of these will become learning that you employ as you progress, developing your expertise and finding your teacher persona.

Your teaching persona is central to establishing your authority and you will need to construct it. Your teacher persona is the version of you that appears when you teach. Experienced teachers have refined this persona and you will observe them 'switch it on' when they teach. Your teacher persona is constructed from your professional behaviours, your responses, your self-regulation, your use of voice and language and the relationships that you establish with students.

REFLECTIVE QUESTIONS

Pay attention to your mentor's behaviour both outside and within the classroom and note:

- How is their behaviour different in the two settings?
- Is their use of language different?
- How do they use their voice?
- Has their body language changed?
- Is their use of humour the same?
- How are they employing gesture?

Authority, then, arises from how we operate in the classroom and our teaching persona, both of which take time to establish. We have also established that effective working relationships are key to building mutual trust and respect. Let's look now at a case study that explores how challenging behaviour and teacher–student relationships might impact.

CASE STUDY: THE IMPORTANCE OF WORKING RELATIONSHIPS IN ADDRESSING CHALLENGING BEHAVIOUR

A teacher, Ms Sartori, who has some experience in challenging environments, joins a school in which the bulk of students are motivated to learn and in which behaviour management is less of a challenge than she has been accustomed to. She teaches music to a Year 9 class that has a mixture of strong personalities. Some are keen to engage with the subject, some are not. One boy in particular represents a real challenge. We shall call him Matthew. He slows down the beginning of the lesson each week by arriving late, waiting for the inevitable challenge and then arguing with the teacher. He is often asked to leave the room before the learning begins, at which point he can become very angry.

In whole group settings, Matthew is loud, assertive and confrontational. He likes to interrupt and likes to challenge the teacher's knowledge of her subject. In small group settings, Matthew dominates the other students and ensures that no learning happens. They are not scared of him; he just keeps them off-task through hilarious clowning. During individual work, Matthew insists on questioning everything and will frequently opt not to work, saying the lesson is pointless. He has enlisted a sidekick, whom we shall call Chris. Chris is silently uncooperative. When Matthew needs someone to engage with his antics, he looks to Chris for an encouraging laugh. When he needs support, he ensures that

(Continued)

Chris is involved in his misbehaviour. This is the catalyst he needs to get the whole class responding as he wants.

The result of this behaviour is that Ms Sartori dreads the lesson each week. She becomes irritated with Matthew very quickly and this can escalate the confrontation. Endless 'telling off' and angrily imposed sanctions seem to be having no effect and Matthew is making no progress whatsoever. The relationship between the two of them is increasingly acrimonious. To compound the issue, the lesson is being disrupted to such an extent that students are becoming disengaged as they witness this power struggle every week, mainly because Matthew is winning; he has far less to lose. Ms Sartori struggles on in this way for a whole term and her sense of dislike for Matthew grows – it is evident for the whole class to see. One of them even asks her, 'Miss – do you hate Matthew?' She tries various sanction-based approaches, but none of them has any effect and her carefully managed teacher persona is breaking apart as her patience is challenged again and again.

In desperation, she turns to the Head of Year for help. Fiercely independent and proud of her experience in challenging environments, she perceives it as a sign of weakness, but has the good sense to recognise that she needs support. Inevitably, the Head of Year asks why she has not spoken sooner. The Head of Year then proceeds to outline Matthew.

Matthew comes from a large family that lives in a 'Red Hot Spot' of social deprivation. Matthew has two brothers in prison and his older brother was permanently excluded from the school two years previously for a violent assault on a younger student. Matthew's mother is a single parent, and his dad's whereabouts are unknown. Matthew's academic profile suggests that he has above-average ability in most curriculum areas, but his attitude to learning varies wildly from subject to subject. Matthew often has conflict with teachers. He has very poor attendance, which amazes the music teacher, as he has been in every lesson she has taught. He has exceptionally low self-esteem, is quick to tears and has a talent for art.

The Head of Year offers to mediate a conversation between the teacher and Matthew. In the meeting, both explain their perception of the lesson. Ms Sartori notices the visible respect that Matthew has for his Head of Year. She is surprised (and annoyed) to learn that Matthew thinks she is singling him out for negative attention and believes that she doesn't like him. She begins to understand (with some indignance) when Matthew explains that, from his perspective, all she does is tell him off and give him detentions. However, he does tell her that he likes her lessons, as they are 'fun'. Ms Sartori swallows her pride, then calmly and deliberately tells Matthew about her frustrations. He appears to listen. They make an agreement to behave in certain ways and to follow some agreed rule systems. The Head of Year advises on some successful strategies from other teaching staff and Ms Sartori leaves feeling much more positive as she considers that some of the barriers have been breached. On reflection, she realises that this is the first conversation she has had with Matthew that hasn't been a response to his challenging behaviour.

The strategies included finding an opportunity to start the lesson with a positive interaction, as well as some clear reminders about expectations. Matthew was given jobs and thanked for completing them. Matthew was praised for being on time. Matthew's positive contribution (however small) to the previous lesson was recognised, privately at first in a quiet aside, but later more publicly as the relationship progressed. Matthew was given tasks that he could succeed in, and the tasks developed in challenge as his confidence grew.

Reminders about expectations were calmly provided every time Matthew began to behave inappropriately, followed by Matthew being given a choice about his next steps. He didn't always make the right choice and, as a result, sanctions were applied, which Ms Sartori took care to impose without raising her voice and remaining as calm as she could. Matthew was clear about what to expect in terms of sanctions and gradually began to accept that there were rules he must follow.

Matthew was denied his audience. Every time he began to be publicly confrontational, Ms Sartori deflected quickly by saying that this would be discussed at a later stage, using her own voice and body language carefully to de-escalate the tension and establishing control over the topic of conversation. She would then return to the conversation at a time and place that supported a positive outcome, speaking with him assertively, but deliberately and constructively, even when he was struggling to manage his own emotional responses.

This was no magic bullet. Matthew continued to flare up quite often, but Ms Sartori kept her side of the deal. Over time, she found herself beginning to relax, even chuckling at his clowning and building a tentative rapport with him. She engaged Chris in the learning early in each lesson and subtly severed the tie that had been causing so much damage. This was not difficult, as Chris really enjoyed the attention. When Matthew arrived in a difficult mood, she learned to spot the signals and dealt with them assertively, but sensitively. There were still outbursts, there was still occasional confrontation, but the frequency and severity of these incidents reduced over time and some mutual trust was established. Ms Sartori was consequently able to strengthen her authority in the classroom as Matthew's behaviour was managed and the class developed confidence in her ability to lead.

Matthew took GCSE Music. Ms Sartori was concerned about this, and even more so when he appeared on her class list for the following year (so did Chris). The different group dynamic and style of learning helped the situation further and despite continuing to be challenging each and every lesson, Matthew made progress and his motivation built over time. Ms Sartori understood the subtleties of his behaviour and a warm working relationship developed between the two of them as he progressed. At the end of the course, Chris and Matthew approached the teacher and gave her a card. Inside was a moving thank-you message in which they referred to her 'brilliant' teaching and in which they apologised for being idiots in Year 9. Matthew gained a grade 4 at the end of the course.

The *Core Content Framework* states that, 'Building effective relationships is easier when pupils believe that their feelings will be considered and understood' (Department for Education, 2019: 26).

The lessons from this case study are clear. Fostering a positive relationship, based on the understanding of individual student needs, is essential for effective behaviour management. Getting the balance right between praise and criticism is critical, and sanctions are more effective when they are imposed objectively, rather than angrily. It is imperative that you manage your own behaviour very carefully. Making use of the information and structures available in your school is also essential. Schools in recent years have made huge improvements to their information sharing systems, but there are still a number of teachers who don't make effective use of the information provided. Sit down and do your research before meeting a class. Know your students. Teach the students, not the room.

EXPECTATIONS AND CLASSROOM CULTURE

Classes are groups. There are up to 35 of them and one of you, possibly with some support if you're lucky. Within that group, there will be established norms. Some of those norms may be helpful to you when teaching. For example, they may have learned elsewhere in the school that they should line up outside the classroom sensibly prior to entry. Some of the norms will be unhelpful. For example, there may be an unhealthy social hierarchy in the group that means some students feel unsafe to speak up. Conformity is a powerful thing (Sunstein, 2019).

If you meet a group at the beginning of their learning journey together, for example in Reception or Year 7, many of these norms will not yet have been established. At this point, the job of establishing the norms that you want to see can be much easier, depending on who is in the room. In essence, you have a blank slate upon which to create.

Mostly, however, you will meet groups who have already established their group identity. You may hear these groups being spoken about in staffrooms. They may be described as difficult, or even the 'worst class in the school'. What teachers mean when they say such things are twofold. First, there are some individuals in the group who present challenge, and that most teachers have found or find them challenging. Second, the social culture within the group makes them difficult to teach collectively.

Depending on the age of the students, some classes will have an awareness of their reputation – they may even be proud of it. They may be invested in their identity, fuelled by the critical and frustrated comments of teacher after teacher, and may have come to believe that they are a collective force to be reckoned with.

Responding to this attitude by creating a different culture is one of the hardest jobs in teaching, but it can be done. Establishing a new culture is about establishing a new set of values and that is done by being clear about what those values are, how they are achieved and, perhaps most importantly, why they should be considered valuable, and therefore aspirational.

Begin by being absolutely, unequivocally clear about what your expectations are. Set out your expectations for the lesson overall, but also plan and communicate them for each stage of the lesson. Be prepared to reiterate your expectations time and time again, and prepare your response for when it is challenged. An example might look like:

- At this stage of the lesson, we are working in silence for five minutes – that silence starts now.

Wait for that silence to start, and once established, respond quickly, decisively and calmly to those who don't follow that expectation. You can't do this unless you know what that response will be, so make sure you have planned it. Be prepared to be tenacious in not letting things go. If you allow students to ignore your expectations, you are allowing them to define the culture. Remember: this is your classroom.

REFLECTIVE QUESTION

- What expectations will you articulate to the classes that you will be teaching? Write some down and think about how they might be communicated succinctly and with clarity.

Follow up success with explicit recognition and praise. This might look like:

> Well done guys, you managed five minutes in silence there. And do you know what I noticed? The work you've produced is so much better. Asif, can you share what you've come up with please, because you produce such excellent work when you're focused.

In following these processes, you are reshaping the collective identity of the group. As they experience success, and do so as a result of meeting your expectations, they begin to reconceive their experience of the lesson and the means by which they achieve positive outcomes. They stop seeking disruption as a form of fun and begin to aim for success. This may sound unlikely and somewhat idealistic, but being part of an effective, successful group or process is highly rewarding – help them to see that.

This is about consistency, endless reinforcement and patience. Accept that it will take time and is linked closely to building effective relationships by establishing mutual respect and trust. All of this is based upon your capacity for ensuring that the rules are followed. How do you do this?

RULES, BALANCE, CONSISTENCY AND TOLERANCE

The ability to respond well to transgressions of rules is critical to your developing success as a teacher. All schools have rule systems and teachers are expected to use them. In many schools, this will take the form of a structured consequence system. Alongside the consequences, most of these systems also outline a rewards system, with the two working in tandem. Much of this arises from Behaviourist thinking. The Behaviourist movement was established early in the 20th century. The concept of operant conditioning (Skinner, 1976), which formed the template for much practice in mid-20th-century schools, involved both negative and positive reinforcements working in tandem to secure desired behaviours. Essentially, and put somewhat simplistically, we can foster the increase of desired behaviours through reward, and foster the decrease of undesired behaviours through sanction.

REFLECTIVE QUESTIONS

- How important is the balance between positive and negative reinforcement?
- What are the likely consequences of too much emphasis on just one of them?

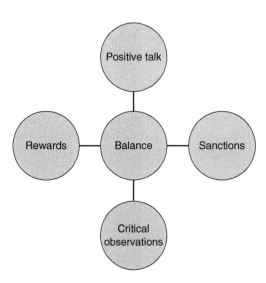

Figure 8.1   Striking a balance between positive and negative reinforcement

Seek to balance out your response, both in terms of rewards/sanctions and the dialogue you establish with the class about their conduct (Figure 8.1). Always aim for more of the positive than the negative, but remember, kids are wise. Too much praise and too many rewards dished out for every tiny success undermines their real value – they need to be worked for. Too many instructions, warnings, critical observations and sanctions lashed out for every minor transgression and they may start to feel that you don't like them, which is a natural human response to being told you are not good enough. This will impact on their self-esteem, their sense of self-efficacy in your lesson and eventually their emotional and behavioural response to your teaching.

What happens when, despite your best efforts, students continue to behave in a manner that falls short of expectations? On one level, the answer is simple, escalate your responses using the school systems until you secure compliance. Be consistent, be openly and visibly fair, be calm, depersonalise your responses, offer choice as you do so, but be prepared to use the tools that the school has given you.

All well and good, but what about students who consistently break the rules every lesson, despite your use of the sanction systems. Should you then aim to respond to every transgression, even if that means them being removed from your lesson each and every time? Is it not desirable that you should modify in order to help those students experience some measure of success?

At this point there arises the concept of zero tolerance. Tom Bennett (2020) states that there is no such thing. He's right. Zero tolerance means responding to each and every rule overstep in exactly the same manner, each and every time. How can such a thing work when there will always be exceptions? If the school rules state no lateness to lessons and that a detention must be awarded, what happens when a student is late because they were chased by a bully and had to hide? If the rules state that incomplete homework means a detention, should that detention be imposed if a student spent the night locked in their room, listening to domestic abuse? The answer in both cases is clearly no – this would be an injustice, would be counterproductive and, consequently, a massive waste of everybody's time, not to mention the likelihood of fostering a negative view of school for the student. Pointless. To state 'no exceptions' is to state the impossible – there are always exceptions.

In our case study about Matthew, to what degree should Ms Sartori enforce the rules consistently? We might think about this in terms of choice and motivation. If Ms Sartori can establish that Matthew is deliberately seeking to disrupt the lesson, then it would be entirely appropriate to respond with sanctions and to do so consistently. If, however, Matthew witnessed the arrest of a family member that morning that involved violence, it is understandable that his emotional self-control might be shaky and that outbursts or non-compliance might result. How should Ms Sartori respond then? Should she, based on her sound knowledge of Matthew, his life and circumstances, seek to understand and then modify her response accordingly? She would still need to address the behaviours, but she would need to do so in a way that responds to Matthew's needs. Bennett, in his excellent book, *Running the Room* (2020), makes the point that the rest of the class needs to be helped to understand why these modifications take place. Sometimes they understand already, and in a case like Matthew's, they may be quick to support him by explaining to Ms Sartori what happened to Matthew that morning. The message here is that it is possible to be both consistent and flexible. As you get to know your students, you will develop your skill in deciding what's appropriate in any given circumstance, and you will also learn to modify in a way that doesn't undermine your authority.

SELF-REGULATION

In the main, we have focused in this chapter on the behaviour of students. What about the behaviour of teachers? How important is your own behaviour in securing an ordered classroom? The answer is that it's absolutely critical. The *Core Content Framework* states:

> The ability to self-regulate one's emotions affects pupils' ability to learn, success in school and future lives. (Department for Education, 2019: 26)

Teachers who don't self-manage impact negatively on students. If students feel that teachers don't care about them, have an active dislike for them, or if they are scared of a teacher's volatile responses, there is very little chance of mutual trust or respect being established. The basis for this thinking lies in the concept of psychological safety. If we don't have psychological safety, we are unlikely to function well. Our sense of psychological safety is affected by the behaviour of others, which can prevent us from making contributions if we feel that it will incur a negative response. In particular, it can affect our readiness to learn (Clark, 2020). These ideas gain further traction if we accept what Maslow told us about our sense of safety being paramount to optimum functioning. His hierarchy of needs outlines how this works in tandem with our other needs, both physical and emotional (Maslow, 1943).

Teachers who shout and bawl at students might ensure compliance (with those meek enough to find this scary), but they are not establishing respect and they are not creating optimal conditions for achievement. In fact, they are demonstrating that disrespectful behaviour is the way to get what you want and they are creating an atmosphere in which many students will struggle to succeed. Some students will respond to this by shouting back, or worse. When questioned about it later, they might state: 'Well, she was shouting at me, so I did it back'. Touché. The only time when shouting is acceptable is if it is needed to ensure safety and to ensure it quickly, or if the class is so noisy that your voice needs to be raised above them. In both of these circumstances, it needn't be aggressive.

There is quite a large space between being assertive and being aggressive or scary. Seek to be firm, but don't seek to intimidate (which is utterly pointless with some students). Seek to be clear, but don't seek to be bombastic. Seek to secure compliance, but don't seek to force compliance. In this way, mutual trust and respect are built.

There are many teachers in school whose behaviour management is highly effective. They achieve this without shouting, without aggression, without exasperation, without labelling and without humiliating students. When you are on placement, find the opportunity to watch these people teach and you will quickly realise that the best behaviour management is achieved by role-modelling. Teachers who embody the behaviours that they wish to see in their students are highly effective because they live the classroom culture that they want to create. The *Core Content Framework* reinforces this explicitly:

> Teachers are key role models, who can influence the attitudes, values and behaviours of their pupils. (Department for Education, 2019: 9)

STRATEGIES FOR SUCCESS

In this section we will look at some strategies for success.

GATHER YOUR INFORMATION

The information you have at your disposal in relation to behaviour and classroom management is significant. Most schools will employ systems that enable you to work both proactively and responsively in this area.

Many schools will employ an information database designed to support teachers in their classroom practice. The organisation of the information contained therein will vary substantially across institutions, but the content will be largely the same and will contain some or all of the following.

SEATING PLANS FOR CLASSES

Some software allows teachers to design and record their seating arrangements. Some of this software also has a provision for recording teacher notes, assessment data and other relevant information. Sometimes seating plans may have been arranged for behaviour or classroom management purposes and you may be able to use the templates that they have created for particular groups. It may be helpful to discuss the rationale for particular seating plans with other colleagues who have the same groups.

(Continued)

ADVICE AND GUIDANCE REGARDING STUDENTS WITH PARTICULAR BEHAVIOUR-RELATED NEEDS

Schools may make advice and guidance regarding students with certain behaviour-related needs available electronically. You may need to access a file, which may be stored in learning support, with a class teacher or senior leader in primary, or a Head of Year in secondary. If the work has been undertaken in cooperation with the student and has drawn on a number of professional inputs, these information sources can be incredibly beneficial. The information from the sources may provide strategies which have proven to be successful. The guidance may also articulate situations that are likely to elicit a negative response from the student. If you know that you have a potentially challenging student in a class you are about to teach, draw on the experience of others and use this information to plan your preventative strategies.

INDIVIDUAL STUDENT REPORTS

Individual student reports sent from the school to parents can provide valuable insight. These vary in detail – they may be purely numerical, they may contain lengthy prose, they may be a combination of both – but schools in both the primary and secondary sectors report to parents regarding behaviour-related outcomes in school. The reports may be articulated using language such as 'Attitude to Learning' or 'Engagement', but they tell a similar (although not exactly the same) story. Key questions to ask yourself include: What does this report tell me about this child? Is the picture consistently the same across all subjects? If not, why might this be? Where does this student enjoy success? Who should I speak to as a result?

SPEAK TO KNOWLEDGEABLE COLLEAGUES

Colleagues with specific roles will be able to support you in understanding the needs of your students better. In primary, the class teacher will have a wealth of knowledge to share, but you might also speak to senior leaders, teaching assistants, subject specialists (depending on the size of the school), playground supervisors and the SENDCO. They will all have insights to share that you might find beneficial. In secondary, a student's form tutor is an excellent starting point, but you might also speak to other pastoral staff, such as those working in support units or withdrawal groups (where these exist) and the Head of Year. Do bear in mind that each of these individual people will be sharing their perspective on that child and that you may hear conflicting information, so make up your own mind as you form a working relationship with students.

REFLECTION AFTER THE LESSON

- Which stages of the lesson went well in terms of behaviour?
- Which stages were more problematic?
- What are the implications of this for my choice of learning strategies with this group?
- At what point exactly did things start to go wrong?
- What happened just before this: can I identify a trigger?
- Were any of the seating arrangements creating pockets of disruption?
- How did I react during instances of disruptive behaviour? Could I have behaved differently?
- When did students react most positively and enthusiastically? What was happening at the time?
- What have I learnt about individual students today? Do I need to modify my own behaviours or my approach in future?
- What are my key learning points to take forward to the next lesson?

TIPS FOR EFFECTIVE CLASSROOM MANAGEMENT

KNOW YOUR STUDENTS AND TEACH THEM AS INDIVIDUALS

- If you understand the people you are working with, you are better equipped to meet their needs. If you meet their needs, they are more likely to respect and trust you.

REMEMBER THAT YOU ARE IN CHARGE, BUT THAT RELATIONSHIPS MATTER

- You can be in charge and be respectful at the same time. Be a leader, not an enforcer. Tell them what you want from them – this is not a negotiation – but do so in a way that communicates the value of making the right choices.

HAVE ROUTINES FOR ENTRY TO AND EXIT FROM THE CLASSROOM

- Establish a routine and stick to it. Whether that's lining up outside the classroom, coming in and standing behind desks, coming in and preparing equipment or coming in and doing a starter activity, stick to it. Students feel comfortable with

(Continued)

routine and you set the tone for the start of the lesson, managing the entrance explicitly. In some schools, this is decided for you. Establish a similar routine for the end of the lesson.

BE EXPLICIT ABOUT YOUR EXPECTATIONS AT EACH STAGE OF THE LESSON

- If students don't know what the rules are, how can they follow them? Say them and display them, then be prepared to issue reminders. Make this a habit and students will be able to repeat back what is expected. Think about your expectations for each stage of the lesson. Are they working in silence individually, or are you allowing some work-related conversation? Is this just in pairs or on tables? Do you need to be clear about not turning around or shouting across the room? How and when will you make this clear?

TAKE THE REGISTER IN SILENCE

- It's an effective means of creating a controlled start to the lesson. It also means that you can be sure that the record is accurate, which has safeguarding implications.

LATENESS - DON'T LET IT DISRUPT THE LEARNING

- If students come in late, sit them straight down and carry on teaching. Don't allow it to disrupt the learning. Make it clear to them (and the rest of the class) that you will be discussing their lateness with them at a later stage. Once the class is engaged with an activity, speak to the students. They may have a good or a private reason for being late, so speaking to them individually affords them a discreet opportunity to explain without the whole class listening. If they are late without good reason, use the sanctions at your disposal consistently.

READ, UNDERSTAND AND ABSORB YOUR SCHOOL'S BEHAVIOUR POLICY

- You can't use it effectively if you don't understand how it works.

AIM TO OFFER PRAISE AT LEAST AS MANY TIMES AS YOU OFFER CRITIQUE

- Ideally, aim for twice as much praise as critique. It impacts positively on culture and it builds trust and mutual respect.

USE TONE-MATCHING TO DEFUSE CONFRONTATION

- If a student raises their voice to you, speak at a volume lower than theirs.

RESPECT STUDENTS' PERSONAL SPACE AT ALL TIMES

- For most people, personal space is at least an arm's length. Getting too close, particularly in volatile situations, can cause defensiveness and result in students feeling threatened.

IF A STUDENT IS BEHAVING IN AN AGGRESSIVE OR AGITATED MANNER, CONSCIOUSLY USE GESTURE TO CALM THEM

- Don't point and don't clench your fists. Step backwards with the palms of your hands showing.

AVOID DEFLECTION: CONTROL THE CONVERSATION BY 'REROUTING' BACK TO THE BEHAVIOUR AND BE PREPARED TO REPEAT YOURSELF

- Students may try to deflect from their behaviour by challenging the rules, challenging your behaviour or challenging your response to other students. This may look like: 'We're talking about the fact that you're not in your seat. I will ask you again – please return to your seat.' Repetition may be necessary.

TALK ABOUT THE BEHAVIOUR, NOT THE STUDENT

- Avoid labelling students. Don't refer to them as disruptive, defiant or aggressive. Refer instead to their behaviours. Rather than saying 'You are so disruptive', say instead: 'This behaviour is disrupting the lesson and we all need it to stop.'

OFFER CHOICE WHEN RESPONDING TO DISRUPTIVE BEHAVIOUR

- In situations when behaviour is challenging, hand them back some control so they can 'save face' and make the right decision. Whatever the situation, offer them their

(Continued)

alternatives and then give them time to make the decision. The temptation will be to remain there staring at them. Do the opposite, give them the choice and then behave as though you expect them to do the right thing. Work with another student for a minute and see if they have had enough time to calm down and move forward.

USE PROXIMITY AND CIRCULATION AS A MEANS OF SILENTLY COMMUNICATING YOUR EXPECTATIONS

- Standing near to an area of low-level disruption may be enough to encourage them to stop. Equally, giving an instruction and then moving away as if you expect them to respond positively works well.

PLAN FOR POTENTIAL SCENARIOS BASED ON YOUR STUDENT KNOWLEDGE

- Try to plan ahead for students with challenging behaviours. If a student does or says this, what will be my response? Do I need support? How will I get the support I need quickly without further disruption? Having these responses ready for incidents with volatile students gives you the space you need to respond to the behaviour without also problem-solving your exit strategy at the same time. It is good practice to include such strategies in your planning while on placement.

PLAN A FANTASTIC LESSON: ENGAGEMENT IS 90% OF THE MISSION ACCOMPLISHED

- Poorly planned lessons nearly always lead to disruption on placement.

ACT WITH ABSOLUTE RESPECT TOWARDS YOUR STUDENTS AT ALL TIMES: DEMONSTRATE HOW YOU WANT TO BE TREATED AND BUILD MUTUAL TRUST

- Model the behaviours that you wish to see from your students.

PRACTISE HEIGHTENED SELF-AWARENESS AND MONITOR YOUR OWN RESPONSES

- Learn to understand your triggers and learn to manage them.

AIM FOR A BALANCE OF CONSTRUCTIVE CRITICISM AND PRAISE

- Too much criticism creates a negative atmosphere and working culture. Too much praise where it is not merited undermines their perception of your judgement.

USE NON-VERBAL SIGNALS TO ESTABLISH QUIET

- Be explicit about their function (teach this) and then use them consistently. A raised hand, followed by the students raising theirs, could be an explicit signal for quiet.

GIVE WARNINGS THAT QUIET WILL BE REQUIRED SHORTLY

- Verbally count down 3-2-1 while signalling with your fingers. Pitch your voice so that it can be heard and deliver in a tone that anticipates students will respond appropriately. It is a request, yes, but one that you expect them to follow.

LOOK FOR AN OPPORTUNITY TO USE REWARDS TACTICALLY

- Rewards can be used to build motivation and to signal successful attitudes to learning. Aim to use them as much as you can, but only give them when they're deserved.

ONLY REWARD EFFORT, BUT YOU CAN CELEBRATE ACHIEVEMENTS

- Rewarding achievements without context can be undermining, especially for those who struggle to achieve. However, it doesn't mean that individual achievements can't be recognised and celebrated. Simply focus on the habits and strategies that led to it, as this is something all can aspire to.

IF YOU MAKE A MISTAKE OR RESPOND INAPPROPRIATELY, APOLOGISE

- This does not undermine you; it builds respect. We are all fallible.

SUMMARY

In this chapter, we have covered:

- Establishing positive behaviour is about your understanding of your students, the working relationships that you establish, mutual respect, mutual trust and very clear expectations.
- High-quality planning is needed to ensure high-quality engagement. This reduces the likelihood of disruptive behaviour.
- A positive learning culture is shaped by the teacher, who is in charge of the classroom. A teacher must be explicit and show the students what is expected. A good teacher will aim to persistently encourage and demand the best behaviour until it is secured.
- Rules must be explicit in order to be followed. A classroom where the rules are spoken but not lived is not effective. Be prepared to repeat the rules and be prepared to ensure that they are followed. Aim for consistency in your responses to all students, and be fair and transparent in your decision-making.
- Consistency is vitally important, but there will always be exceptions. Knowing your students is the best way of determining if an exception needs to be made. If you make an exception, support the class in understanding why, if this is possible.
- Punishment alone will not secure good behaviour or good learning.
- The way that a teacher behaves sets the tone for the class. Exemplify and role-model the behaviours that you wish to see in your students.

REFERENCES

Bennett, T. (2020) *Running the Room: The Teacher's Guide to Behaviour.* Woodbridge: John Catt Educational.

Clark, T. R. (2020) *The 4 Stages of Psychological Safety: Defining the Path to Inclusion and Innovation.* Oakland, CA: Berrett-Koehler Publishers.

Department for Education (2011) *Teachers' Standards.* London: HMSO. Accessed online (23 February 2021) at: www.gov.uk/government/publications/teachers-standards

Department for Education (2019) *ITT Core Content Framework.* London: HMSO. Accessed online (23 February 2021) at: www.gov.uk/government/publications/initial-teacher-training-itt-core-content-framework

Maslow, A. H. (1943) A theory of human motivation. *Psychological Review,* 50(4), 370–396.

Skinner, B. F. (1976) *About Behaviourism.* New York: Vintage Books.

Sunstein, C. R. (2019) *Conformity: The Power of Social Influences.* Albany, NY: New York University Press.

9

SUPPORT STRUCTURES FOR STUDENTS

IN THIS CHAPTER, WE WILL COVER:

- What are the different systems used to support students?
- How can you be an effective form tutor (secondary) or class teacher (primary)?
- Which roles are specifically designed to provide additional support to students and how do they work?
- Which external agencies can offer additional support to students?
- What is safeguarding and what are your statutory responsibilities for keeping children safe?
- What do we mean by 'mental health' and how can you support young people with this?

INTRODUCTION

Support systems come in many guises. They might be described as 'Attitude to Learning' systems, guidance, student support, well-being, home-base. The list can be long, but they all serve the same purpose – to ensure that the students in the school are given the right support and incentivisation to succeed in their studies.

How, when and for what reason a student makes use of these services varies according to need. In most secondary schools, students can access these systems via their form tutor (where forms exist) or, on occasion, via a subject teacher. In primary schools, it can be a class teacher or a specialist teacher. Having said that, students may present difficulties to or confide in any member of staff on site, and everybody has a duty of care to ensure that they are listened to and appropriately supported. Management structures are often designed to reflect the fact that schools both deliver an academic programme and offer a more general support package to their students. Part of this structure is the role of the form tutor and/or the class teacher.

THE FORM TUTOR AND CLASS TEACHER

This section uses the term 'form tutor' when referring to a range of roles. While this is most likely to be applicable terminology in a secondary school, the intention here is to provide guidance to colleagues working in support roles with a group that they see frequently. Some secondary schools don't use the term, and most primary schools don't. It can therefore apply to class teachers, home-base tutors, registration tutors or any other configuration of the role in both the primary and secondary sector.

During the placement stage of your training, it is likely that you will be attached to a form. During your Early Career Teacher year, you may be allocated a form of your own, or you may share one with a more experienced teacher.

A good form tutor is pivotal in securing success during a student's time at school. Each school will articulate the expectations of the form tutor, but given the quite personalised nature of the role, the way in which these expectations are carried can vary considerably. In many ways, it relates to the reasons why people choose to become a teacher in the first place.

REFLECTIVE QUESTIONS

- What duties might a form tutor or class teacher be expected to carry out?
- In what way do you think this role impacts on students?

During my role as a teaching assistant at the very start of my career, I formed the somewhat simplistic view that you were either a teacher of your subject or you were a teacher of children. What I was attempting to articulate was a sense that some teachers only really focus on the subject matter without really concentrating on the humans in the classroom. You can probably see the beginning of the journey towards the guiding principles here. Simplistic though this view was, there was a nugget of truth contained therein.

Put very basically, you will struggle to be an effective form tutor if you don't engage with and enjoy the personalities of the students in your form. Although form time is short in the secondary sector, there is plenty of opportunity for you to add the more personal touch to the work, even if the duties you are expected to carry out are numerous. The best form tutors don't just treat this time as checks and monitoring that need to be completed; they build relationships, build a form identity, communicate expectations, set the day up (if the session is first thing in the morning), solve problems, offer support, chivvy, encourage and hassle, organise just about everything, and act as the first friendly professional face of the day.

In primary schools, the early part of the morning is an opportunity to do all of the above as well, and you may be lucky enough to work in a school where you spend the majority of the day with the group as well. One key element, in both sectors, is to check at the start of the day that everybody's well-being is such that they can engage with the day's learning. Be vigilant. Mental health is covered in more detail later in this chapter.

As well as somehow squeezing all of this in, schools are increasingly expecting tutors to make structured use of the time. Ofsted now visits form rooms to assess the effectiveness of the provision. They are looking for focused, purposeful and constructive activities. Some might argue that this is valuable social time, but it is not the world we live in, so try to find a balance between allowing the students a slightly less formal and enjoyable start to the day and ensuring that you can demonstrate that the time is being used to support their engagement with school life. So, what might this look like?

- Checking diaries/planners
- Monitoring homework completion/organisation/rewards/behaviour. (sometimes done electronically using software like SIMS or Classcharts)
- Running a quiz on current affairs
- A short presentation on something topical or philosophical, followed by a debate
- Students presenting on an area of their life outside school
- Reading time, with discussion about the books
- Study time
- Structured reflection on homework/revision/effort/targets
- Competitions
- Prize giving/celebration activities
- Charity work
- Literacy or Numeracy activities
- Percussion session

This is just the beginning of an endless list – be creative with the time. To do this, though, you have to plan.

As time progresses and your form begins to trust you, it is likely that they will start coming to you with their problems and will be seeking advice. At this point, it is important to recognise two things:

- You can't solve every problem that you are presented with
- Somebody else might be able to

To coin a phrase, you are not alone. Developing an understanding of the support structures within your school and those available outside the institution helps you to carry out your role more effectively. Let's have a look at this within school to start with.

REFLECTIVE QUESTIONS

- How are the support structures within your current school configured?
- How are these different from when you attended school?

SAFEGUARDING

Every member of school staff has a specific responsibility to ensure that children are safeguarded. Schools also have a responsibility to ensure that you are trained annually in this area. The training should cover the processes and systems that the school employs, including the school's child protection policy, behaviour policy, the staff code of conduct, safeguarding responses that occur when children go missing in education, and the identity and contact details for the designated safeguarding lead and any deputies.

As a teacher, it is important to be alert to the signs of abuse. As a form tutor or class teacher, you see the same children every day and you are therefore likely to notice if there are any behaviours that might indicate that a child is suffering from harm. Changes in behaviour or appearance might indicate a recent instance of abuse, so be alert for these. However, be mindful that not all changes mean that abuse has occurred. Children undergo changes all the time. If in doubt, speak to a member of staff who has specialist knowledge in this area – it never harms to raise your concerns.

Some abuse may happen because parents, carers or other adults act in ways which harm children. Other kinds of abuse occur when adults fail to take action to protect children or fail to meet a child's basic needs.

There are four main types of abuse:

- *Physical abuse*: This may involve hurting or injuring a child by hitting, shaking, poisoning, burning, scalding, drowning, suffocating or otherwise causing physical harm to a child.
- *Emotional abuse*: This is the persistent emotional ill treatment of a child. It may involve telling children that they are worthless or unloved, inadequate, or valued only insofar as they meet the needs of another person.
- *Sexual abuse*: This is forcing or enticing a child or young person to take part in sexual activities, whether or not the child is aware of what is happening. It may also include non-contact activities such as involving children in inappropriate sexual activities.
- *Neglect*: This is the persistent failure to meet a child's basic physical and/or psychological needs, which is likely to result in the serious impairment of the child's health or development.

Witnessing domestic abuse is also harmful to children.

The NSPCC (2021) has suggested that the following signs might indicate that abuse is occurring:

- Talks of being left home alone or with strangers.
- There is a poor bond or relationship with a parent, also known as attachment.
- Acts out excessive violence with other children.
- Lacks social skills and has few if any friends.
- Becomes secretive and reluctant to share information.
- Is reluctant to go home after school.
- Is unable to bring friends home or is reluctant for professionals to visit the family home.
- School attendance and punctuality is poor, or they are late being picked up.
- Parents show little interest in the child's performance and behaviour at school.
- Parents are dismissive and non-responsive to professional concerns.
- Is reluctant to get changed for sports, etc.
- Wets or soils the bed.
- Drinks alcohol regularly from an early age.
- Is concerned for younger siblings without explaining why.
- Becomes secretive and reluctant to share information.
- Talks of running away.
- Shows challenging/disruptive behaviour at school.

While these are indicators, they do not necessarily mean that abuse is happening. If you have a concern about a child, don't keep it to yourself.

On occasion, you may receive a disclosure from a student. A disclosure is information that leads to concern for the safety of a child. In the event that this occurs, you have some clearly defined responsibilities, as articulated in *Keeping Children Safe in Education* (Department for Education, 2021).

In the event of disclosure, you must not keep this information to yourself and you must not promise the child confidentiality. Your school will have a Designated Safeguarding Lead (DSL). There should also be at least one deputy in this role. It is your responsibility to make them aware, straight away, of the information that you have received. If you are unable to reach them, then you can seek advice from a member of the senior leadership team. If you are unable to do so and have concerns about the safety of a child, it is your responsibility to take advice from social care professionals by contacting the local helpline yourself. Delay can be dangerous for the child, so don't wait until breaktime or the end of the day. The local authority has a responsibility to respond within one working day, although, depending on the nature of the concern, they may respond more quickly.

The most sensible way to approach your safeguarding responsibilities is to ask yourself the question: am I in the slightest doubt about the safety of this child? If the answer is yes, seek immediate support. The worst that will happen is that your concerns are investigated and nothing is unearthed. This is no reflection on you; you took professional responsibility for the well-being of a child.

REFLECTIVE QUESTIONS

- What processes exist within your current school to support the safeguarding of students?
- What is your level of knowledge and comfort in relation to these procedures?
- Do you need additional advice and, if so, whom should you contact?

SCHOOL SUPPORT

Most modern schools invest heavily in their support structures. The link between happy, safe, supported students and high levels of achievement is well established. The manner in which this is structured varies immensely. This variety can depend upon the context in which the school finds itself (geographically), the school's current relationship with the Inspection Framework (most recent judgement), the students that attend (demographically) and the priorities of the leadership team and governors (ethos and culture).

SUPPORT MANAGERS

Most schools are divided into year groups. In the secondary sector, there can be up to 400 students in the largest schools. In smaller primary schools, it may be just a handful of students. Alternatively, the students may be divided into other groups, such as a Key

Stage, or houses that function across year groups. In secondary schools, and in some larger primary schools, a form tutor or class teacher, in terms of line management, will usually sit within such a structure, and might find themselves in a group of as many as 15 other tutors. The next level up is usually a coordinator of a group of forms. This might be a House Head, a Head of Year, a Year Coordinator, a Year Manager, a Director of Progress, a Key Stage Manager – the names vary. The role will usually be undertaken by a teacher, but it might also be a non-teaching member of staff.

These roles can vary considerably. Those that are occupied by teachers are quite likely to have a dual function, whereas those occupied by support staff are generally (but not always) more specifically focused. One of the roles will be to ensure the well-being of the students: this might involve safeguarding; behaviour management systems, including reports, detentions and exclusions; a role in counselling (informally) and supporting those experiencing difficulties; the sharing of information with colleagues; liaison with parents; liaison with some outside agencies; implementing and coordinating reward systems and leadership of assemblies – the list is not exhaustive.

In addition, they may be responsible for monitoring progress and ensuring that the necessary support is in place for those struggling to meet expectations. Monitoring and supporting students will involve an informal information-gathering process that is very much connected to the more pastoral aspects of the role, outlined above. They will also often be the designers of the reporting and evaluation processes following a cohort assessment or reporting point. This will usually involve identifying those who are not doing as well as might be expected and ensuring that this information is shared, as well as designing interventions and monitoring systems to ensure improvements. Those students who are doing well (again this might be defined in numerous ways) will also be identified in this process, so that their achievements might be celebrated or rewarded.

The next tier above in the line management structure is likely to be a senior leader: usually an Assistant or Deputy Head. They will coordinate the work of the pastoral managers and aim to ensure some consistency in the systems across the school. They are often responsible for safeguarding, the design and implementation of key policies across the school, and they tend to be the person involved when a situation becomes very complex and/or challenging. They will be at the 'sharp end' when behaviour results in exclusions, or when a child needs multi-agency support. They will have a detailed understanding of the way in which all the systems and policies are coordinated to provide the very best support for the students, staff and the school.

THE SENDCO

Sitting alongside this structure, in both the primary and secondary sector, will be the critical role of the SENDCO (Special Education Needs and Disability Coordinator). This role is designed to ensure that all students who have additional needs are given the support that they need, and also to ensure that the school meets statutory requirements in this provision. Their key responsibility is to coordinate the Annual Review process for those children entitled to formal support. These reviews are connected to an Education Health Care Plan (EHCP). This plan coordinates provision across different agencies to ensure that a student with significant needs can access the curriculum and the resources across the school site. Students who have fewer challenging needs, but nonetheless require additional support, will also have their needs coordinated by the SENDCO. This will involve the deployment of Learning Support teaching staff and teaching assistants; the distribution of key information to staff across the school; training staff on how to meet additional needs; liaising with external agencies who provide additional support; working with the child and their parents/carers to ensure that their needs are fully understood, then communicated to the right people; and carefully monitoring the provision to ensure that needs are met. More information on this role and provision for SEND students can be found in Chapter 5 on obstacles to learning.

REFLECTIVE QUESTIONS

- Looking at the roles mentioned above, can you envisage yourself progressing in your career to such a position?
- What experience and knowledge would you need to gain to pursue such a role?

OTHER SUPPORT ROLES

As mentioned previously, schools will structure their support systems to meet the needs of their individual context. A list is provided below. Please be mindful that the titles of the roles vary from school to school and sector to sector. Some of the responsibilities will vary as well. Some of these roles might include the following.

ISOLATION COORDINATOR

The isolation coordinator is responsible for managing the isolation/internal exclusion system. They will work in the room with isolated students. Isolation or internal exclusion is often used as an alternative to formal exclusion from school or may be part of a reintegration process. It may also involve some restorative work to enable a return to curriculum provision. They may have a background in behaviour management, counselling or may have worked in corrective facilities.

LEARNING MENTOR/SUPPORT WORKER

Learning mentors or support workers will work directly with students, and provide a range of support strategies. This work could be conflict resolution, workshops with groups covering a variety of topics, somebody to talk to, a safe place, additional subject support, coordination of inclusion processes, liaising with parents, and accessing additional funding and/or support. The titles for the role will vary considerably from school to school.

PUPIL PREMIUM CHAMPION

The increased focus on students receiving free school meals in recent years has resulted in schools being required to evidence effective spending for their Pupil Premium-eligible students. One area of provision that has developed is the introduction of Pupil Premium champions, whose specific role is to support these students. Depending on the size of the cohort and the seniority of the role, they will work to coordinate provision for these students in a similar way to that employed by the SENDCO.

SCHOOL COUNSELLOR

The school counsellor role is growing considerably and is likely to expand further as the government builds the requirement for schools to engage with mental health. These roles vary in their scope and level of expertise. Some schools have an informal counselling arrangement in which they make a member of staff available to provide support. At the highest levels, schools or Multi Academy Trusts might employ a fully qualified counsellor or psychologist to provide support to those students whose need is greatest. Given the scope of mental health issues among children presently, their services are very much in demand.

ATTENDANCE OFFICER

Again, these roles vary in approach, focus and seniority. In some schools, a member of the administration staff might be deployed to monitor attendance and provide data to the relevant colleagues, such as a Head of Year, for example. The next level up from this is a specifically appointed attendance specialist, who would normally gather the data and then be engaged in first-stage responses. The role would usually involve gathering and analysing the data, then distributing it. It might also involve making phone calls home for first day absence and/or speaking to students regarding their absence and chasing evidence to ensure that the student has not truanted.

At the next level, an officer might be employed to design and run interventions designed to raise attendance for specific students or groups of students. These interventions might be triggered by attendance figures or they might be based on direct interaction with the child. There may well be a punitive element for students who are absent without authorisation, or they may meet with parents who have kept a child out of school without authorisation. In terms of support, they might put a coordinated plan together to encourage improvements. Such interventions might involve the form tutor, the parents and other key staff working together. At a strategic level, attendance is usually the responsibility of a member of the senior team, whose role will be to raise attendance across the school and to report to Governors and the Department for Education.

TEACHING ASSISTANTS

Teaching assistants (TAs) provide one of the most vital roles in a school and represent the one role you are most likely to work with frequently. The role has come under some scrutiny in recent years, partly as a result of the work of Professor John Hattie (2012). His research identified that the impact of teaching assistants on learning was not positive. He was, however, quick to point out that it wasn't the role as much as the manner in which TAs were being deployed that was at the root of this lack of impact; it was the result of ineffective partnerships between the teacher and the teaching assistant.

TAs can be incredibly helpful both within and outside the classroom and they can work in a variety of ways. They range in their level of qualification and experience. Some of them will be very highly qualified and you will find they have an immense amount of knowledge and experience upon which you can draw.

TAs are there to support the learning within the classroom. They might have been assigned to support the needs of a particular individual, or they may be in the classroom to support a group. If you are lucky enough to be allocated a TA, then take the time to work with them productively – they may have deep understanding of and expertise about the children. Productive working involves meaningful conversations about planning, to which they can contribute, and also about adaptation, with which they can provide invaluable support during the lesson. The *Core Content Framework* makes specific reference to this role, stating:

> Teaching assistants (TAs) can support students more effectively when they are prepared for lessons by teachers, and when TAs supplement rather than replace support from teachers. (Department for Education, 2019: 29)

This quotation refers to the potential abdication of responsibility by the teacher that occurs when a TA is supporting a particular individual. Poor practice means simply leaving that child to be guided by the TA, without any input from the teacher. Good practice is about effective partnership working. This can be challenging in the course of a normal, busy school week, but the time is well invested and will impact positively on student progress and the quality of your lessons.

EXTERNAL AGENCIES

External agencies work with schools to provide support to students whose needs are the most acute. There have been many attempts by successive governments to coordinate the efforts of these agencies to deliver the best provision for students. Sadly, they have yet to prove effective – mainly because of money. As austerity measures bite yet further, already stretched services find themselves under intense pressure to deliver support in highly restrictive circumstances. Nevertheless, there has been some success out there and some students do get the support they need. The key services with which you might have contact are outlined below.

CHILDREN'S SERVICES

A specialised sub-section of Social Services, this agency provides support to children who are at risk of harm: this is referred to as 'Safeguarding'. Their work is usually coordinated by social workers, who will become involved with a child if certain thresholds are met in terms of their safety.

Children with whom this agency works may be placed on support plans. There are two types of plan: a 'Child in Need Plan' and a 'Child Protection Plan'. Both plans are designed to provide the additional support that some young people may need to ensure their safety and well-being. Such plans might be the result of a referral from a member of staff based in a school, following a disclosure, or a concern being raised.

A Child in Need Plan is designed to support young people who are not at immediate risk of harm, but who may require additional support with their health or development. The plan will involve the child's parents or carers and will take account of the child's background. The plan will articulate what support is required and by whom. It could involve schools or other agencies and it will also include the parents or carers. Clear, time-specific goals will be set.

A Child Protection Plan is the next level and is designed to keep a child safe when the child is likely to suffer harm. It sets out the steps needed to safeguard the child, identifies the key individuals/agencies who will be instrumental in that process, details the processes that those individuals/agencies are expected to follow, identifies the consequences if the plan isn't adhered to, and implements a timetable for securing improvement.

Depending on the circumstances and nature of the plan, and on the nature and frequency of your role in working with the child, you may be informed that the plan is in place. If this occurs, you may be asked to monitor the child's well-being and contribute to the professional conversations that inform the plan. Such work can be challenging and your school should offer you support and guidance in working in this manner.

CHILD AND ADOLESCENT MENTAL HEALTH SERVICES

The role of the Child and Adolescent Mental Health Services (CAMHS), a service within the NHS, is to provide support for young people experiencing difficulty with their mental health or with mental illness. CAMHS can provide support with anxiety, depression, food disorders, self-harm, schizophrenia, bipolar disorder, violence and anger.

Mental health refers to a person's social, psychological and emotional well-being and is distinct from mental illness. Mental health is something that applies to all people and it determines our actions, thoughts and feelings, as well as our relationships with others and our response to stress (NHS, online). Mental health is best thought of as a spectrum: a person is not either mentally well or mentally unwell, but rather they experience a range of responses to their environment at different times.

In the early 21st century, there has been an exponential rise in recorded incidences of poor mental health (Marshall, Bibby & Abbs, 2020). The situation has been further exacerbated by financial austerity, the impacts of the Covid-19 pandemic and social media. Triggers for poor mental health might include poverty, social isolation, discrimination, bereavement, separation, acting as a carer, drug or alcohol abuse, trauma or domestic violence.

Access to the CAMHS service is via a referral. This is usually made by a GP, but it can also be a teacher or a parent/carer, or other involved professionals, such as a social worker. Following the referral, an appointment will be made in which the issues are discussed and then a course of support will be identified. For young people in the greatest crisis, this support might even involve a specifically designed residential environment.

Some children will seek support with their mental health issues; others will not. In your role as a teacher, and particularly in a support role, you are well placed to notice if a child appears to be struggling. The best teachers form meaningful working relationships with young people. Doing so will make you more attuned to the child's behaviour and its potential causes. It will also make it more likely that a child will seek support from you. It will give you greater understanding of their individual context and their potential responses to adversity.

Signs that a child may be suffering from mental health issues are that they:

- have become very withdrawn
- are frequently tearful

- show raised levels of anger and/or irritation
- have altered sleep patterns
- are lacking in energy and seem very tired
- show little interest in food

While you may not witness some of the above during the school day, students may talk about it, either directly with you, or you may overhear it being discussed. It's worth remembering that the list above does not mean that mental health issues are definitely occurring; some of them are behaviours that may present in young people who enjoy good mental health.

There is a lot of guidance material designed to help professionals and parents in supporting young people with their mental health. Take the time to read some of it so you can increase your likelihood of offering appropriate support. The NHS CAMHS website (National Health Service, 2021) is an excellent starting point.

STRATEGIES FOR SUCCESS

This is the section in which we consider some additional strategies that support the focus of this chapter.

GATHER YOUR INFORMATION

When working as a form tutor or class teacher, your efficacy in supporting your students with their needs as well as their learning will be enhanced by knowing your students in more detail.

Seek to foster a meaningful working relationship with parents. Parents (most of them) really appreciate contact from teachers that is proactive and positively focused. Conversations in which you show a genuine interest in a child build mutual understanding and let parents know that you have their child's interests in hand. You can also learn from these conversations. Parents may share information of the kind that isn't recorded on school systems. You may learn, for example, that somebody attends swimming practice at 5am every day, or that a severely disabled family member shares the home, or that they have a famous relative or that their mother is head of a school. All such discoveries help you to understand the student in more detail, foster positive relationships with them, and will also help you to support that young person more effectively. Should you need to contact home for less positive reasons in the future, the conversation is more likely to be productive. This doesn't just apply to your support roles; it is also useful when teaching.

(Continued)

If you find that a student in your class has a particular difficulty or obstacle in life, take the time to do your research. We all have some superficial knowledge about issues such as depression or anxiety, but how much do you really know? Do your reading and seek to build your range of strategies for providing the support that student may need. Vulnerable children need advocates, and as a teacher you are supremely well placed to be one.

Finally, and most importantly, take the time to get to know your class. Open up conversation about their lives, their interests, their hobbies, their views and their experiences. Celebrate their achievements outside school and offer support when they experience difficulty or loss. Doing so will build an inclusive environment in which they can fully present who they are as individuals and feel a sense of belonging. Informed practice will help you to become a more rounded, respected and impactful teacher.

TIPS FOR EFFECTIVE SUPPORT

KNOW YOUR STUDENTS

- Take the time to form meaningful working relationships with students. Show an interest in them as individuals.

DEVELOP YOUR KNOWLEDGE OF MENTAL HEALTH ISSUES THAT YOUR STUDENTS MAY EXPERIENCE

- Attend training and access reading about the different mental health problems that young people may encounter. Develop your strategies based on what you learn.

PLAN ACTIVITIES THAT BUILD THE SOCIAL HEALTH OF YOUR CLASS, WHILE ALSO CREATING A FOCUSED START TO THE DAY

- Don't allow form time or the start of the day to be an unstructured time that creates a negative start to learning.

BUILD A POSITIVE CULTURE IN YOUR CLASSROOM BY MODELLING THE BEHAVIOURS YOU WISH TO FOSTER

- Students are more secure in a room where they are respected, valued and listened to.

CREATE AN ENVIRONMENT IN WHICH MISTAKES ARE SEEN AS AN OPPORTUNITY TO DEVELOP

- Avoid being negative and critical in response to the mistakes your students make. In particular, avoid labelling – we are not defined by the things we get wrong.

AIM TO DEVELOP POSITIVE WORKING RELATIONSHIPS WITH PARENTS OR CARERS

- Engaging parents in learning and the life of the school can be hugely beneficial to students. You build consistency of approach and work to support each other in helping students to succeed.

COMMUNICATE, EXPLICITLY AND FREQUENTLY, HIGH EXPECTATIONS IN RELATION TO CONDUCT AND INTERPERSONAL BEHAVIOURS

- Have an agreed code of conduct for your room. Use the school systems consistently and fairly, building a space that is safe for all, irrespective of background, ability or social status.

REGULATE YOUR EMOTIONAL RESPONSES

- Shouting, angry outbursts, labelling, inconsistent responses, irritability and disrespect will not impact positively or lead to better responses from students.

IF YOU RECEIVE A DISCLOSURE THAT RAISES EVEN SLIGHT DOUBT ABOUT A CHILD'S SAFETY, REPORT IT IMMEDIATELY

- Do not promise confidentiality. Do not try to assess the level of risk yourself. Do not wait until breaktime. Take the immediate steps necessary to support the child.

SUMMARY

In this chapter, we have covered:

- Schools employ a range of internal and external systems for supporting students. One of the key roles of a teacher is to provide this support.
- An effective form tutor or class teacher develops meaningful working relationships with students, support workers and parents or carers.
- An effective teacher makes the effort to be informed about their students and their students' needs.
- All teachers have a responsibility to safeguard students and specific responsibility to familiarise themselves with *Keeping Children Safe in Education* (Department for Education, 2021).
- Mental health refers to our capacity to engage socially, psychologically and emotionally with our environment. The way in which our environment is structured can have an impact on our mental health. Teachers have a responsibility to ensure that their own behaviour, and consequently the environment they create, impacts positively on their students' mental health.

REFERENCES

Department for Education (2019) *ITT Core Content Framework*. London: HMSO. Accessed online (23 February 2021) at: www.gov.uk/government/publications/initial-teacher-training-itt-core-content-framework

Department for Education (2021) *Keeping Children Safe in Education: Statutory Guidance for Schools and Colleges*. London: HMSO. Accessed online (24 June 2021) at: https://assets.publishing.service.gov.uk/government/uploads/system/uploads/attachment_data/file/954314/Keeping_children_safe_in_education_2020_-_Update_-_January_2021.pdf

Hattie, J. (2012) *Visible Learning for Teachers: Maximising Impact on Learning*. Abingdon: Routledge.

Marshall, L., Bibby, J., & Abbs, I. (2020) Emerging evidence on COVID-19's impact on mental health and health inequalities. *The Health Foundation*, 18 June 2020. Accessed online (16 June 2021) at: www.health.org.uk/news-and-comment/blogs/emerging-evidence-on-covid-19s-impact-on-mental-health-and-health

National Health Service (2021) *Children's and Young People's Mental Health Services*. NHS website. Accessed online (13 June 2021) at: www.nhs.uk/mental-health/nhs-voluntary-charity-services/nhs-services/children-young-people-mental-health-services-cypmhs/

NSPCC (National Society for the Prevention of Cruelty to Children) (2021) *Keeping Children Safe*. NSPCC website. Accessed online (13 June 2021) at: www.nspcc.org.uk/keeping-children-safe/

10

PROFESSIONAL DEVELOPMENT: MOVING FORWARD IN YOUR FIRST TWO YEARS

INTRODUCTION

You've made it. You have completed all of your academic assessments and you've passed all of your placements. Your provider has recommended you for Qualified Teacher Status and you are ready to begin employment. It's over.

The fact is, it's only just beginning. You have proved your competency and you are employable (on paper, in any event). Your first few years as a teacher will be challenging and tiring; having said that, they will also hopefully be inspiring, fulfilling and memorable.

In this chapter, we will focus on transitioning from trainee to qualified teacher. We will begin by looking at how to secure your first teaching post, starting with finding your school, then moving on to completing your application and statement, through to some interview tips.

Next, we will look at what you can expect from the newly introduced *Early Career Framework* (Department for Education, 2019). It places responsibilities on both you and your employer. We will discuss how the Framework is designed to support your first two years in post.

Finally, we will consider how you can make the best of your new life, focusing on your work–life balance and making the most of the opportunities on offer.

SECURING THAT FIRST JOB

RESEARCH THE SCHOOL

Begin by choosing your school carefully. Not all schools will be suited to your disposition, teaching style or educational views. Some schools will offer you the opportunity of making a visit. If they do, take it. It shows interest and also gives you the opportunity to get a feel for the place and ask some questions. Lively, motivated and interested candidates have an opportunity to make a positive first impression on such visits. In addition, do a search on the school and find out what information there is in the press. Check the school's website and familiarise yourself with its ethos. Look for the values they express, their key successes and also access the school improvement plan. This research will enable you to talk with confidence about how you might contribute to their trajectory.

REFLECTIVE QUESTIONS

- What sort of a school would you like to work in?
- Will it be urban or rural?
- In an affluent area or an area of deprivation?
- Part of a multi-academy trust or a local authority school?

WRITING YOUR PERSONAL STATEMENT

Personal statements are an incredibly important part of applying for your first teaching post. Think carefully about how you want to present yourself. Make sure that you describe the kind of teacher you are and the one that you aspire to be when working in the school, and do so using lots of enthusiastic, committed language. Check your statement very carefully for language errors – these create a very bad impression. Use a highly competent proof-reader if you need to. Many ITT tutors will be happy to support you with this process. Additionally, don't use the same statement for every school, but rather tailor each one to the findings from your research about the school. Senior leaders who are reviewing applications are looking for potential commitment to their institution.

Your experience is important and should be described in a way that evidences competence. Draw on your previous experiences outside teaching, but don't dwell on them. Use those experiences to demonstrate your competence and skills. Also, use your placements to demonstrate the skills and knowledge you have developed during your ITT year. You can use the checklist in Table 10.1 to help you construct the statement.

Table 10.1 Checklist for your personal statement

Elements to include	Present?✓/X
A clear introduction that states the kind of teacher you are and the one you want to be.	
Describe your work ethic. How do you approach tasks? How would others describe your work?	
A rationale for your application to that particular school – why have you chosen them?	
A description of how you ensure good behaviour and engagement – what routines work well for you and how do you foster positive working relationships? Refer to experience.	
A statement outlining your subject/Key Stage expertise. What do you bring to the team? Refer to academic background and teaching experience.	
Some discussion about learning. What is it, how do you facilitate it and how do you know when it has happened? Refer to experience.	
Your expertise in meeting individual needs, including SEND. Refer to experience.	
Your interests and how these might support/enhance extra-curricular provision.	
Your aspirations and plans for the future.	
Proof-read it, or ask somebody to do it for you. Check for language and positive tone. Look at your paragraphs – are they too long, too short?	

FILLING OUT THE APPLICATION FORM

This next section of guidance may seem a little obvious, but there are many people who make the mistakes that we are about to discuss. The application is about more than just gathering information. It also conveys something about your professionalism. A sloppily completed form with spelling mistakes, missed sections, abbreviated entries, different font sizes or inaccurate responses will result in you being removed from the selection list. I have seen forms completed in this manner for posts at a senior level.

Another element to be aware of is Safer Recruitment. Schools are required to operate very stringent processes when appointing teachers that comply with *Keeping Children Safe in Education* (Department for Education, 2021a). Part of this process is to ensure that an application form contains no unaccounted-for gaps in your history, in which you could have been involved in an activity that would prohibit you from teaching and that you may be attempting to conceal it. It means that you need to ensure that you have accounted for all periods of adult life. Most of this will involve work history and/or education, but you may have been travelling or undertaken other activities. Some application forms will provide you with an opportunity to explain your full history; in others, it is advisable for you to do so in your statement.

INTERVIEW TIPS

Dress like you are serious, turn up early, show enthusiasm for the school, but most of all, be yourself. The day of your interview is a two-way process. You are being interviewed for your fit with the school, but you also have to decide if it is the right school for you, and whether the people in it, as well as their culture and ethos, match the way that you like to work.

Most interviews involve a tour. Pay attention and see what you can learn. It's a good idea to identify a question or two that you can ask later in the interview. This will demonstrate how observant you are. Aim for a question that illustrates that you have understood their ethos or recognised a key strength. Examples might include: 'I noticed that you have a three-strike behaviour system posted on walls around the school. I like systems like this one – do you find it is consistent and effective?' Or: 'The teachers here seem very relaxed when talking to students. Is this a deliberate part of the way that you work?' Or: 'All of the students are dressed very smartly in their correct uniform, how did you achieve this?'

Think about the questions that you will be asked and prepare your answers. For an Early Career Teacher (ECT) post, you will almost certainly be asked about the following subjects:

- How a teacher secures good behaviour and/or engagement
- What an outstanding lesson looks like
- How learning happens

- How to adapt your teaching to meet individual needs, particularly SEND
- How you use formative assessment
- Why you want to work at that particular school
- Where you see yourself in five years' time
- What you can offer in addition to teaching
- Your key qualities
- One thing you need to change/improve
- A successful/unsuccessful lesson that you have taught

It is a good idea to prepare some scenarios for answering these questions. Behaviour for learning is much easier to talk about if you connect it to a successful lesson in which you secured high levels of engagement. SEND is easier to discuss if you can provide an excellent example of when you have supported a student.

REFLECTIVE QUESTION

- Think about some examples of effective work you have undertaken. Which of these would make good examples for you to draw on in interview?

You may be asked to teach. Some of these sessions can be very short (20 minutes or so). Make sure that you have planned carefully, and for the shorter sessions in particular, it's important not to be overly ambitious. Your observer will be looking to see how you interact with the class and how you set up a learning environment. In terms of the learning, be absolutely clear about what you want the students to achieve in your time together and find a way of demonstrating to your observer that the class has met the success criteria. Keep it simple and be explicit about the learning at each stage of the process.

Many interviews also include a student panel. The most common mistake made in such processes is that the candidate speaks patronisingly to the students. This can manifest as being irreverent or doing a lot of 'telling'. Look to foster a quality conversation. Be open, be respectful and be aware that this group will have a voice in your selection process.

Trainees who are successful in interviews are those who are successful on the course. If you can demonstrate that you have been developing well as a teacher, can show an enthusiasm, energy and willingness to continue developing, and an awareness of your own strengths and areas to improve, and can demonstrate that you have immersed yourself fully in the life of your placement school, you will be successful in securing a role (although be prepared for the fact that this may not be in your first interview).

One final piece of advice is to think about what will give you the edge. Is there a club you could run or is there potential for you to teach another subject or bring an area of specialism to the school?

Once you have secured a role, you will take on the status of an Early Career Teacher and the good news is that you will be entitled to continued support as you start your new job.

THE EARLY CAREER FRAMEWORK

The Early Career Framework (ECF) was rolled out nationally in 2021. The ECF (Department for Education, 2019a), along with Statutory Induction (Department for Education, 2021b), articulates the entitlement for Early Career Teachers (ECT) as they enter the first two years of their career following qualification.

The ECF has been implemented as a response to recruitment and retention issues within the profession. It has been widely publicised that large numbers of teachers leave the profession within five years of starting. There are many who have not yet left but who are planning to do so. The Department for Education hopes that, through providing an additional package of support and some time for professional learning to take place, these numbers will be reduced.

YOUR ENTITLEMENT UNDER THE ECF

Schools are required to provide you with training, a reduced teaching load, a mentor and an induction tutor. The requirements placed upon schools can be found in the Induction Guidance from the Department for Education (2021b). Note that the guidance is statutory, which means that you are entitled to this provision and that schools are required to deliver it.

The training can be provided by the school, or they can purchase it from identified external providers. The aim in using external providers is to ensure consistency in quality and content.

You will be assessed in two ways: formal assessments at the end of each term and progress reviews in terms where no assessment takes place. It is not dissimilar to the process you undertake during your ITT year, although it occurs far less frequently. The framework for your assessment, as in ITT, will be the standards. The *Core Content Framework* (CCF) (Department for Education, 2019b) and the Early Careers Framework are not designed for assessment purposes. Each term, you will set objectives based on the *Teachers' Standards* (Department for Education, 2011), but these may draw on the 'Learn that…' or 'Learn how to…' statements contained with the ECF. In addition, at the end of each academic year, a formal assessment will also be submitted by the school. The process should be a dialogue; you should not be told at the end of a year that you are not going to pass. If issues do arise with your progress, the school should be putting support and intervention in place as the year progresses. The guidance states that there should be no surprises.

While there is no explicit requirement for you to build an evidence base that demonstrates you are meeting the standards, it would be wise to identify, as you progress, the key pieces of evidence to which you, your mentor and your induction tutor might refer. The guidance is clear that the process should not create extra work for you as an ECT, but also states that referring to evidence will be a means of carrying out assessments. The easiest way to demonstrate your development is simply to keep a folder into which you put all of your evidence of good practice as you go along.

Your mentor, who must hold Qualified Teacher Status (QTS) themselves, will be the person with whom you will work most closely in this target-setting and review process. They will meet with you on a regular basis and provide coaching that supports your development. They are likely to be specialist in either your subject (secondary) or phase (in primary). The school is required to provide them with sufficient time to carry out this role. They will work in a very similar way to your ITT mentor.

Your induction tutor will be responsible for your overall assessment and for submitting the relevant documentation. They are likely to be a senior member of staff, and unless you are in a very small setting, they will be a different person from your mentor. They are required, as part of the process, to observe you at regular intervals during your first two years, but you may also be observed by other colleagues as part of the process. It is important that these observations are fully supportive, and the guidance stipulates the following:

- The ECT and the observer meet to review any teaching that has been observed, with arrangements for post-observation review meetings made in advance
- Feedback from the observation is provided in a prompt manner and is constructive, with a brief written record made on each occasion; and any written record will indicate where any development needs have been identified. (Department for Education, 2011: 21)

If your observer follows these key principles, the observation process is likely to be more supportive and more useful to you as a developing teacher.

With regard to your teaching load, the ECF is explicit. You must receive a 10% reduction in your first year, and a 5% reduction in your second. Broadly speaking, this means two additional free periods in year 1 and one in year 2 (depending on your school's timetable). However, schools are likely to interpret this in different ways.

This process, if delivered according to expectations, should provide the support that you need to progress beyond your ITT. The leap from ITT to ECT is quite significant, but this new process is much better placed than previous models in supporting teachers who are newly qualified. Let's look forward now to how you can make best use of this time and also look after your well-being as you do so.

YOUR FIRST YEAR IN POST

Your first year as an ECT will be just as challenging as your ITT year. This may not sound terribly positive, but it does get easier as you progress from this point forward. The main challenge will be the increase in teaching load. Moving from 12/13 lessons a week to 19/20 is quite a step up.

Alongside acquiring those extra lessons, you now also acquire extra responsibility. Your classes – their progress and engagement – are now your responsibility. Although this may add to your sense of pressure, remember always that you are part of a team. No teacher is required to work in isolation. At the least, you will have your mentor and induction tutor, and in most environments, you will find yourself working alongside supportive and developmentally focused colleagues who are more than happy to help. There is nothing wrong with seeking advice, asking for help, or just looking for a supportive conversation.

Stress and fatigue are likely to be features of your first year, and they can affect people in different ways. As you get to know your class or classes and familiarise yourself with new systems and processes, it is not unusual for those new to the profession to feel tired and a bit overwhelmed. The well-being of new colleagues has a much sharper focus than it once did, and there should be plenty of people with whom you can discuss your issues, should they arise. There is no shame in stating that you need support, and it should not reflect on your professionalism or sense of efficacy; we all struggle at points and we are all human.

Find a way to make it work for you. Pay attention to when you are most productive. Most teachers have a metacognitive sense of their own productivity. Some will tell you that they work best early in the morning when very few people are on site. Others prefer to work in the evening, once they are sufficiently relaxed. We can all learn more about ourselves, so notice what works for you. Use your weekends to recharge. There may be some work to do as well. You will know yourself best. Will it be better to leave it until Sunday night or would you feel more relaxed if it's out of the way first? Establish some routines that work best for you and aim to stick to them, but also be prepared to give yourself a break when you really need it.

Try not to be the person who works from 7am to 11pm. It is important to relax and this is best achieved through realistic planning. Planning your day, and your working week, will help you to achieve a balance. Learn to manage your expectations of yourself. One of the things teachers often say is that the list is never-ending – you can never reach the end. This may not always be strictly true, but do try to accept that you can't do everything at once. Work out what your priorities are and which things can wait until a later stage. Talking to experienced colleagues about these issues is invaluable. They are experienced, and have lasted in the profession precisely because they have learned how to make it all work.

Your first year in teaching should be, on the whole, an incredibly valuable and rewarding experience. You can really settle in with your classes and into the school as a whole, becoming a valued member of the professional community. As your teaching continues to improve, you will experience some inspirational moments as you watch students progress, as well as some moments of difficulty, which are best shared with colleagues. You will develop some fantastic working relationships with both students and colleagues, and you will see the impact of your work in the classroom, which is incredibly rewarding.

Being an active part of the wider community can really enhance this sense of belonging and your sense of contribution. Look to involve yourself in life outside the classroom where time permits. Schools have such a varied programme outside lessons and there are plenty of great opportunities to get to know students in a different setting, as well as to collaborate with peers. Getting involved in clubs, trips, revision programmes, extra duties, sport, the arts, professional development programmes or just social events will really improve your sense of well-being and enjoyment as the year progresses. Finally, get some sleep.

REMAINING DEVELOPMENT FOCUSED

We will finish this chapter by thinking about your future, and specifically, how you retain the habits and mindsets that characterise an effective professional teacher. Let's begin with two short case studies.

CASE STUDY 1: A STRUGGLING PROFESSIONAL LIKELY TO FAIL

Ryan, a teacher from Leeds, was struggling in his role as a French teacher. Results were poor and he had been placed on a development plan to improve his practice following an observation by senior leadership. Part of his support package was to be assigned a mentor (Lucy) who was outside the management structure.

Lucy met with Ryan several times. She found that Ryan did not agree with the assessment of his practice. He felt he was doing much better and was being targeted by management unfairly. During the meetings, Ryan did most of the talking while Lucy listened. She noticed that most of his talk was focused on how unfair his situation was, how difficult teaching is, how challenging the students are and that management didn't understand how to teach languages. Lucy was patient, sought to empathise, but also sought to develop some of his thinking so that it was more development focused.

Lucy offered advice and guidance. She suggested helpful reading, introduced new strategies, analysed data and outcomes, and managed to persuade Ryan, slowly, that

(Continued)

---

some changes would support his work. She worked to co-plan a lesson with him and they arranged an observation.

Lucy then watched Ryan's lesson. He set the class some textbook reading and then sat with his back to the class checking his emails. After a period of time, he stood and went through a PowerPoint presentation, talking for 20 minutes, pausing to ask two questions that had little relation with the learning. The students, throughout the lesson, appeared disengaged and when Lucy spoke to them, were unable to articulate their learning. Not surprisingly.

When Lucy shared her thoughts on the lesson, Ryan disagreed with her findings, defended his choices, explained that she didn't understand his workload and, the next day, requested that Lucy be replaced by somebody else.

CASE STUDY 2: A STRUGGLING PROFESSIONAL LIKELY TO SUCCEED

Sanna, a trainee teacher working with a Year 6 class, was finding behaviour management really challenging. She was in an inner-city primary and the students had a range of needs. She was visited by her ITT tutor who identified some specific issues around her approach and then shared these in feedback following an observation.

The lesson had been particularly challenging and Sanna was very upset. After recovering, she listened carefully to the feedback and sought to understand what the key issues were. She took professional responsibility for the situation in the classroom and accepted that it was her task to make the changes that were required. Some of the guidance provided previously by her school mentor had not been specific enough to help her move forward, but she did not seek to hold the mentor responsible. She and the tutor discussed that professional dialogue and recognised that the mentor was diligent and supportive.

Sanna went away and read the material recommended by the tutor. She sought further discussion with the mentor, involving her and continuing the dialogue that she would need moving forward. She observed an experienced colleague, who also provided further guidance. She developed new strategies, including them in her planning and sharing them with both the tutor and her mentor. There was healthy debate between the three of them about the new ideas and they refined them collaboratively.

Over time, Sanna worked with the challenging group and supported them in improving. Her own work improved as she did so and she began to really enjoy the progress and engagement that was being secured in the room. At the end of her placement, she was assessed as outstanding.

THE STANDARDS AND PROFESSIONAL DEVELOPMENT

The *Teachers' Standards* contain some very specific descriptors that pertain to these case studies. In Standard 8, the sub-standards state:

develop effective professional relationships with colleagues, knowing how and when to draw on advice and specialist support

and

take responsibility for improving teaching through appropriate professional development, responding to advice and feedback from colleagues (Department for Education, 2011)

These two descriptors may sound very obvious, but it is usually the case that teachers who lose their development focus are the ones who start to underperform. It is often characterised by an unwillingness to accept feedback and a lack of drive in securing improvements.

Teachers who remain open to new learning, new ideas, feedback, coaching and mentoring are the ones who develop into truly outstanding professionals. A teacher's role is to support learning; if teachers are not willing learners themselves, this is likely to impact on their capacity to facilitate it in others.

In Chapter 3 on learning, we discussed mindsets, based on the work of Carol Dweck (2006). A teacher with a growth mindset (one who works on their sense of self-efficacy and believes it can improve) is one who is much more likely to foster this in others. Sanna, in case study 2, invests trust in her colleagues, accepts that change is both necessary and is within her power to secure, and then takes the necessary steps to get there.

As you progress in your career, pay attention to your own mindset and challenge yourself to remain focused on improving. Really great teachers embark on the learning journey with their students, do so openly, sharing their metacognition and communicating their enthusiasm and energy for the process. This is infectious and the impact in the classroom is profound. Be the role model that your students need.

STRATEGIES FOR SUCCESS

This is the section in which we consider some additional strategies that support the focus of this chapter.

RESEARCH A SCHOOL THOROUGHLY, BEFORE MAKING YOUR APPLICATION

- This could include looking at the website, Ofsted reports, media reports, the school performance tables and by making contact for an initial conversation about the role.

(Continued)

THINK CAREFULLY ABOUT THE KIND OF SCHOOL THAT YOU WANT TO WORK IN

- A school that is high-achieving or one that is struggling with results? An urban, suburban or rural school? An outstanding school or one that is moving forward? Large or small? Private or state? Selective or comprehensive? Progressive or traditional? An academy or a local authority school?

PREPARE A DESCRIPTION OF YOUR TEACHER IDENTITY

- Who are you when you teach? What is your style? What kind of working relationships do you establish with students and colleagues? Do you aspire to leadership? What are your key strengths?

COMPLETE THE CHECKLIST WHEN COMPLETING YOUR PERSONAL STATEMENT

- Have you covered all of the areas that you need to cover? Have you presented yourself in the most positive light possible? (Refer to Table 10.1)

ENSURE THAT YOUR PERSONAL STATEMENT ADDRESSES THE JOB DESCRIPTION PROVIDED AND IS SPECIFIC TO THE SCHOOL TO WHICH YOU ARE APPLYING

- A generic statement will not secure you an interview.

PREPARE SOME ANSWERS AND SCENARIOS IN ADVANCE OF YOUR INTERVIEW

- Think about potential questions and how you might answer them. Think about examples of good practice that you can draw on to illustrate how effective you are as a teacher.

IF YOU ARE ASKED TO TEACH IN INTERVIEW, KEEP IT SIMPLE AND DON'T BE OVERLY AMBITIOUS

- Stick to what you know. Make the success criteria explicit and then seek to demonstrate that the students have met those criteria.

SEEK OPPORTUNITIES TO INVOLVE YOURSELF IN THE WIDER LIFE OF THE SCHOOL

- Run clubs, participate in trips, offer extra tuition and participate in continuing professional development (CPD). This will evidence your enthusiasm but also enable you to develop your skills and your professional relationships.

IF YOU'RE STRUGGLING, ASK FOR HELP

- Nobody can be expected to be 100% effective, 100% of the time, and you shouldn't expect it of yourself.

PAY ATTENTION TO WHEN YOU WORK BEST

- Work–life balance is best achieved by paying attention to what works best for you. When are you at your most efficient and effective? Use what you learn about yourself to plan your working week in a way that allows you some relaxation.

REMAIN OPEN TO FEEDBACK AND LOOK TO IMPROVE YOUR PRACTICE

- Teachers who are willing to learn, who are open to critique, who read and who develop professionally are the best teachers.

SUMMARY

In this chapter, we have covered:

- Employers are looking for well-informed, proactive, diligent, professional teachers who will contribute meaningfully to their school.
- Personal statements and application forms are your opportunity to demonstrate all of the above – give them the time and attention they deserve.
- Interviews require research and preparation. Make sure that you understand the school and that you have thoroughly prepared both your answers and your lesson.
- The ECF is designed to support you through your first two years in teaching. It is both your entitlement and the school's obligation to you.
- Professional relationships will be crucial in securing your success in your first two years. Do what you can to contribute meaningfully to the team.
- It is OK to find the job tiring and stressful. Many do. Be open with your colleagues and build your networks of support.
- You will have to work towards a healthy work–life balance. Seek advice and pay attention to what works for you.
- Remaining development focused and adopting a growth mindset to your professional practice will impact profoundly in the classroom.

REFERENCES

Department for Education (2011) *Teachers' Standards*. London: HMSO. Accessed online (23 February 2021) at: www.gov.uk/government/publications/teachers-standards

Department for Education (2019a) *The Early Career Framework*. London: HMSO. Accessed online (2 June 2021) at: https://assets.publishing.service.gov.uk/government/uploads/system/uploads/attachment_data/file/978358/Early-Career_Framework_April_2021.pdf

Department for Education (2019b) *ITT Core Content Framework*. London: HMSO. Accessed online (23 February 2021) at: www.gov.uk/government/publications/initial-teacher-training-itt-core-content-framework

Department for Education (2021a) *Keeping Children Safe in Education: Statutory Guidance for Schools and Colleges*. London: HMSO. Accessed online (24 June 2021) at: https://assets.publishing.service.gov.uk/government/uploads/system/uploads/attachment_data/file/954314/Keeping_children_safe_in_education_2020_-_Update_-_January_2021.pdf

Department for Education (2021b) *Induction for Early Career Teachers (England)*. London: HMSO. Accessed online (10 June 2021) at: https://assets.publishing.service.gov.uk/government/uploads/system/uploads/attachment_data/file/972316/Statutory_Induction_Guidance_2021_final__002____1___1_.pdf

Dweck, C. S. (2006) *Mindset: How You Can Fulfil Your Potential*. New York: Random House.

CONCLUSION

This book has been designed to help you make your way through your ITT year and some of it will also be useful as you progress in your first post. At this point, it is useful for us to review some of the key takeaways from your reading.

Hopefully, you have gained a sense that effective teachers work with young people in a way that celebrates their individuality and supports it. Reducing students to numbers, categories or labels, or placing a limit on what you might expect from them, based on assumptions, is not helpful.

Mutually respectful working relationships, based on sound knowledge of young people, their circumstances, their obstacles, their interests and aspirations, are the bedrock of effective partnership working.

Teaching is a highly skilled profession and requires a wealth of specific knowledge. Neither your skill base nor your knowledge base will ever be complete. The best teachers remain focused on their own professional development and are characterised by a desire to continually improve their practice.

Teaching is demanding and rewarding in equal measure, but the levels of demand and reward are constantly in flux. Learn to be highly organised and proactive. Look after yourself: a teacher who is well in themselves is best placed to support young people. Be honest with yourself: ask for help when you need it. We can't all be perfect all of the time and nobody is expecting you to be. Mistakes happen and we all have our low moments.

Young people going through the process of growing up are facing huge levels of challenge in the 21st century. Be kind to them, seek to understand their needs and model the behaviours you would like to see. At the same time, be prepared to establish your expectations and to work in securing them.

Professionalism is all about making your contribution a positive one. Be on time, be prepared, be proactive and take responsibility for your actions. If you get it wrong, recognise your errors and move forward.

Schools are full of experts. Some of these are teachers, some are support staff and some are students. Consult, listen carefully and act upon what you learn. These people know what they're talking about.

Your energy, enthusiasm and knowledge are infectious. Look to inspire, motivate, build curiosity and bring fun to the learning. Seek to know your students, teach them individually and pay attention to their learning.

If you manage, over time, to build some of this into your professional practice, wonderful things might happen. You may be at the centre of young people opening their eyes to the world and all the possibilities that it offers. Watching that process occur and being part of it is what teaching young people is all about. I wish you luck... and you might need it!

INDEX